BOG-STANDARD BRITAIN

QUENTIN LETTS

Constable • London

First published in the UK by Constable,
an imprint of Constable & Robinson Ltd, 2009

ISBN: 978-1-84901-120-4

Printed and bound in the EU

1 3 5 7 9 10 8 6 4 2

Dedicated to my defiantly English father
and my ceaselessly optimistic mother

Contents

Acknowledgements

Acknowledgements to Andreas Campomar, the *Daily Mail* library, my wife Lois, Maddie Mogford, Maggie Pearlstine, Gina Rozner and Gill Watmough.

Introduction

I will lift up mine eyes unto the hills: from whence cometh my help.

Psalm 121

A wet yuh up wid di Maggy.

Jamaican rap singer Vybz Kartel

All men are not equal. Some are born stronger than others and it is their duty to help the infirm. They will not do this by hiding like milksops. Leaders do not galvanise a frail citizenry by trembling behind matron and saying, 'Ooh, I'm no better than anyone else.' False modesty debilitates a society. Lack of grandeur will benefit only our enemies.

Inequality exists, full stop. A few people are good at maths, many not; a handful can run for miles, the rest of us develop a stitch after a couple of hundred yards; some have a flair for carpentry, others are no more able to assemble an Ikea table than the Masai warrior, plucked from his mud hut, knows how to play 'Blankety Blank'. Unfairness – and, with it, a sense of gradation – is inevitable. Children born to a doctor are likely to be healthier than children born to unmarried mothers in drug dens. The silliest response is to try to deny this truth. The second silliest response is to suggest that low grade is somehow more desirable. Only the daftest romantic thinks it must be preferable to be reared in sink-estate Manchester than gravel-drived Hampshire. The rough slum may well craft a more resilient person but would any of us actually choose that over the more comfortable option? You'd have to be mad – wouldn't you? – to argue that the more fortunate child should renounce its culture and aim to live like a less privileged person. This, however, is what has happened in Britain in the past fifty years. Our rulers have tried to discard the excellent in much the same way the young Tony Benn renounced his viscountcy. The elite has sought to deny its existence. In trying to show (admirable) sympathy for underdogs it has celebrated the crass and the grotty by flattening its accent, coarsening its culture, by jumping down in the gutter with the thick and the violent, the sexually incontinent, the drugged, the criminal, vexatious, cruel, indolent, selfish and unpatriotic. In doing this, our elite thought it was doing the decent thing. Alas, it was simply betraying the very people it aspired to help: the ambitious, blameless poor.

We are losing the idea of citadel, a notion of what is best and what is worth acquiring. If people have no sense of what is best, how can they improve themselves? In the past half-century our leaders have vetoed the idea of a British national character, shying away from it because they were terrified of sounding jingoistic. Policy-makers attempt, above all else, not to sound classy. Yet a culture without a strong, identifiable, porous elite – a group with recognisably higher manners and ideals – is a culture ripe for the swamp.

In these early years of the twenty-first century, 'class' is used to attack a caricature of high-falutin' indulgence. It has become a nasty word, devoid of comedy or warmth, a concept attended by black clouds and threatening chords. Were it a character on the stage, Class would wear a swirling cape and speak with a Vincent Price accent. Class would be some sort of lah-di-dah grotesque and come to a sticky end.

Defenders of crisply enunciated English on the BBC are told they are 'toffs'. Once the T word is deployed, well, no further argument is deemed necessary. Class consciousness is held to be a sin. Aristocrats are beyond contempt. To be a titled nobleman is almost worse than being a sex maniac or a drug fiend or a rip-off merchant who robs widows and orphans. Spouters of orthodox opinion flourish the charge of class prejudice, confident that they have, with that one accusation, sealed victory. Their tone of voice as they do so is almost that of a contestant on Radio 4's *I'm Sorry I Haven't a Clue* when saying 'Mornington Crescent'. Class warfare taps home the victory like Theo Walcott's instep. Class is the clincher. But this class neurosis lowers standards. It spreads mediocrity. It permits pre-Victorian levels of coarseness to pollute our streets. Intervene? No, that would be an act of class prejudice. Opprobrium has been driven from our public life. Shame and propriety and judgements of right and wrong are replaced by whispered orthodoxies about what is 'appropriate', codes which can be understood only by sociology graduates. Manners have disappeared, to be replaced by strict 'guidelines' about sexism and racism. Classy people once knew instinctively how to behave. Now manners have to be taught in rehabilitation classes. They have lost their humanity and become 'codes of conduct'.

Traditional ideas of honour have been dumped. A Home Secretary siphons £116,000 out of the public purse for a dodgy second-home allowance. Within days it is stated by a New Establishment investigator that the minister has 'not broken the rules' and is therefore free to go about her business. Minute legalese has bypassed an obvious impropriety. A society with a stronger grasp of class might have recognised that the minister was misbehaving, but small print has trumped class morality.

Commissions, working parties, think tanks, steering committees, conferences, charities, consultancies: egalitarianism has become an industry for the self-righteous, a largely secularist employment belt whose own high priests think themselves unbelievably important. In the past twenty years it has grown beyond anything envisaged by the socialist Fabians or even by their communist cousins. If the dotty old Webbs, Beatrice and Sidney, came back to Britain today they would be horrified by this behemoth of privileged paddlers. They would ask: where is the good, here, for our poor? The equality world has become a self-feeding monster, a job creation scheme for the clerical caste. Tokenistic equality now commands state policy on everything from broadcasting to front-line warfare in a foreign field, where British human rights have been ruled to hold sway, at least on our side of the trenches. *Dakker-dakker-dakker* chats the enemy machine gun. *Boom* goes a mortar. Smoke fills the air. 'Sorry, Sarge,' the platoon's shop steward is now legally entitled to say, 'but me and the boys ain't attacking that Taliban position until a proper risk assessment has been filled in and handed to the appropriate line manager.' The decency of the lion-hearted British infantryman ensures that this has not yet come to pass but a few ambulance-chasing lawyers working on the egalitarian principle of no-win-no-fee might soon change that.

From university admissions to unisex hospital wards, equality runs like bindweed, strangling common sense. Officialdom towers over us, wagging its disapproving finger, instructing us to observe equality codes or face the withdrawal of public funds. Even the selection of candidates for our Parliament might have to comply with equality edicts, single-sex selection lists already being in operation in some parts of the system. The political elite has made 'access' its specialist subject. There *will* be equality, even if the majority does not want it. 'One man one vote' has been nuanced to 'one man one vote provided we have first been allowed to skew the ballot paper'.

The language heard on airwaves is smudged by egalitarian neurosis. The content of our museums, the plays staged at our theatres, even our sporting ideals – all these quake before the great god equality, the constant, highly politicised impetus towards populism – in short, bog-standardism. In this remorseless process, old gauges of elitism are held to be unacceptable. Beauty fades. Excellence withers. This strips away our cultural dignity, our sense of what it is, or was, to be British because egalitarianism can tolerate no difference in taste. Egalitarianism speaks Esperanto. Egalitarianism sings the *Internationale*. Egalitarianism hates the Queen's English.

Despite all this, equality has not achieved its aims. Social mobility is dropping. The wealth divide broadens. 'Equality practitioners', as they call themselves, have simply become a new super-pod, brahmins amid the beggars, sixth-form monitors of thought who draw their salaries from the pockets of the very poor they profess to help. Egalitarianism, like too many toys on Christmas morning, sounds good and comes with glitzy packaging but does not actually work. Urban babyboomers' terror of social difference has been a disaster. It was born of the social destruction of the Thatcher years, when paternalism was snapped, and is now fuelling a communal obsession with the creed (and for too many people now the lucrative occupation) of equality.

No less an egalitarian than Alastair Campbell, Tony Blair's malevolent henchman, once referred in a loose off-drive to 'bog-standard comprehensives'. Bog-standard Britain. You said it. Mate.

Part I
Communications

Jonathan Dross

Let us open our inquiries with a question. Jonathan Ross: how come? How come this man is the best-paid person at the BBC? How come he receives so much airtime? With that ineffectual voice and those jowls it is a surprise he ever made it past the first screen test.

You will know of his misdeeds. He asked David Cameron if, as a youth, he had masturbatory fantasies about Mrs Thatcher. He said he was 'worth a thousand BBC journalists'. He took part in a puerile stunt with a comedian called Russell Brand which involved them teasing elderly actor Andrew Sachs about his sexually active granddaughter. BBC executives defended Ross as a 'great talent' but he isn't, particularly. He is only mildly amusing. Pretty average, really.

Ross is no creative maestro. His humour is, in tone and format, derivative and his delivery is self-congratulatory, what we can perhaps call London self-referential. His humour is narrow in age range and he cannot sing, dance or play an instrument to any notable level. And yet he is the best-paid star of our national broadcaster. Millions of pounds are squirted into his bank account every year. Why?

When BBC executives called him a 'great talent' it was because they were under attack and wanted to justify the continued employment of this coarse 48-year-old (as the conservative commentator Charles Moore has noted drily, Ross is older than President Obama). Beeb high command was feeling got-at, and got-at is never a comfortable position for a quasi-civil service. To that extent the defensiveness was understandable. However, it also showed the resistance of the corporation's controllers to licence-payer opinion. They plainly felt that the public and the tabloid press were being small-minded. They felt they knew better than the little people.

In today's Britain few people in authority bother much about decency. They recoil with high-minded horror from anything that smacks of racism or sexism, but when it comes to old-fashioned manners, well, this is the twenty-first century. Who cares about the odd swear word and sexual reference? I was going to say 'innuendo' but innuendo is old hat. Nowadays they go straight for the neck. It is not thought improper to swank about copulation and to use the F word on air. There is little hesitation about causing offence unless it be on some matter concerning equality. Boy, they make up for it then.

Ross is employed at vast cost because he is held to have the voice of the people – that is, the section of the populace liked and recognised by BBC producers. The corporation's ill-shaven director-general and his lieutenants are in hock to the demotic. They think that the only way they can continue to lift the licence fee from the pockets of the British public is to appeal to low taste, mainly of the twenty-to-thirty age range. When seeking a top presenter they therefore look for someone who will impress recent college leavers, children of the destructive Thatcher years, the fashion and iPod crowd. Jonathan Ross, though himself on the cusp of his sixth decade, is such a creature. He has never grown up, talks fluently about pop culture and 'movies', has a default setting of urban sarcasm and speaks English with sloppy imperfection. There are plenty like him. One thing you will never hear said about Jonathan Ross is 'they threw away the mould after they made him'.

For the cloistered Jesuits of Television Centre, Ross reflected the Britain they thought they should attract: the informal unmarrieds, the retail junkies, subsidised, self-regarding, inexpert. Ross is very much a generational Pied Piper, representative of an age group which has never quite shed late adolescence. Here is a man of stunted scepticism (he is a sucker for Hollywood PR). He is dead to considerations of religion, tradition and nationality, seeming keener on America than on his own country. Come off it, you say, the bloke's only a light entertainer. But that is not quite true, is it? With his film reviews he is one of our more prominent arts critics. He fancies himself a socio-political campaigner, promoting his studio singers 'Four Poofs and a Piano' as some sort of equality gesture. They were reasonable musicians but would they have landed the gig under a different name? Hard to say.

Ross could be much better but chooses not to be. For all that air of blokeish half-competence he is well educated and was raised in comfort. He comes from a showbiz clan and read history at university. He is plainly intelligent and has a solid family life. So why does he goof around with jerks like Russell Brand? Why does he spatter his act with profanity? Why gurn and gawp and grin like a man half his age? Why so mediocre?

I'm afraid it is because, like the leaders of a BBC which has lost grip of the public service ideal, Ross is a follower rather than a leader. He settles for reflecting the society round him rather than trying to improve it. He could do cerebral but that would not sell. There is more moolah in moronic. The man is an appeaser of fashion, a windsock, a jellyfish on the tide. Until he goes it is hard to see how the BBC can regain public esteem and aim for the more elevated tone which may be its only hope of survival.

The S Word

Words change. Take 'snob'. A snob used to be a cobbler's apprentice. That aproned grunt toiling in a fug of leather glue, sweeping tacks from the workshop floor and occasionally thwacking his thumb with a persuader: he was the snob. Like most apprentices, the snob tended to go up in the world. Aspiration was the fuel of his achievement. He knew that if he worked hard and behaved well and observed certain rules of social congress and kept his hands off his neighbour's ox and his ass and his servants and his wife, well, he could prosper and one day own his own shoe repair business. Later to be bought up by the Timpson's chain, no doubt.

In eighteenth-century Cambridge, 'snob' was applied to townies (as opposed to the college gownies). The word has an abrupt, pungent flavour yet there must have been plenty of people – the publicans of Fitzwilliam Street or the lower bourgeoisie's plump-bosomed wives – who said, 'I'm a snob and proud of it.' Quite right, too. *Vive la différence.*

Rank should never dominate our lives. We should be its master. We need not accept the station to which we are born but should settle for the level that makes us happiest. Those 'snobs' of Cambridge would not have thought themselves worse than the young men in the colleges. They surely relished their own identity.

The late art historian James Lees-Milne, a fragrant Herbert who spent the middle of the last century creeping round large country houses for the National Trust, observed a nice difference between class distinctions and class barriers. Class distinctions were, he thought, the 'chief ingredient of the world's greatest fiction'. Class barriers he disliked greatly. Lees-Milne was right. Class barriers will eventually result in the protected class becoming atrophied but class distinctions allow us to measure ourselves against the rest of society and work out where we are best able to bobble along like a cork on the sea. They offer rewards for self-improvement and a caution against self-neglect. They are our social speedometer and enable us to keep within the limit best suited to our engine capacity. Sadly, this is rare in modern Britain. Our country has been hijacked by a compulsion to homogenise society, to control individualism and turn us all into one classless soup. This puritanical tendency is found chiefly in the dogmatists of the privileged, miserable Left. It is stupid because it stops us making the best of ourselves. It also runs against every human instinct. It is actually anti-social. Socialism is about communal values and they are best nurtured when the community comes together in its various parts. Force-fed egalitarianism is more likely to force people into ghettoes – or 'gated communities', if you live in certain parts of the Home Counties.

The better-off feel persecuted and refuse to become confident leaders of society. Theatre programmes usually carry lists of benefactors. It is depressing how often these generous souls prefer to be called 'Anonymous'. You could argue that this is merely British modesty but there are two reasons for giving money to a good cause. One is to help the cause pay its bills. The second is to set an example. Class ambition helps us to improve

our behaviour, or at least it used to before the levellers arrived
with their bulldozers.

You can no more outlaw inequality, and snobbery, than you
can outlaw BO on a crowded London Underground train in high
summer. No group was more aware of status and minutely
calibrated seniority than the Politburo of the old Soviet Union.
Oh, baby, the bitching that used to occur about the placements
on the Kremlin balcony for the May Day military goosestepathon.
Gordon Brown is equally alive to the power of the political snub,
the almost Japanese pecking order of the high political class. So
why do they try to hide it? When Alan Milburn was announced
as a big figure in Labour's 2005 general election planning team,
Mr Brown threw his rattle out of the pram, so infuriated was he
that one of his rivals had been promoted. To hear lectures from
such a privileged son of the Manse about the wicked defects of
elitism is, well, a very rum business. It is almost as good as the
recent squabbles inside the Equality and Human Rights
Commission, where the chairman, Trevor Phillips, was accused
of not showing leadership. But my dears, we thought you disliked
that sort of thing!

As far as the word 'snob' goes, the 1933 Shorter Oxford English
Dictionary, edited by Onions, states that by 1852 a snob was 'a
person belonging to the lower classes of society; one having no
pretensions to rank or gentility'. And yet by 1859 it was used to
mean 'a vulgar or ostentatious person'. From pretension to
ostentation is the most human of steps. Ostentation, with its petty
qualms about fish knives and what to call the crapper, is certainly
not the prettiest of traits. But social mobility would not exist
without pretension because without pretension we would simply
settle for the lot into which we were born. We would give up, stew,
moulder. That way, no one would ever budge an inch socially and

we'd be back to the worst of pre-Industrial Revolution serfdom. So let's hear it for ostentation. A little more social preening and self-betterment might actually be good for us all.

The very term 'social mobility', so beloved of egalitarians, is an acknowledgement of social differences. Leftwingers drone on about mobility from low to high, but it can also happen in reverse. Look at the likes of Lord Brocket, a rather thick hereditary peer imprisoned for insurance fraud, or Lord Archer of Weston Super Mare, gaoled for perjury, or even Sir Fred 'The Shred' Goodwin, the high-flying Royal Bank of Scotland chief executive who one month was feared by his underlings and fêted by the media, only for everything to vanish a month later when it turned out he had driven the bank to the brink of ruin. Goin' down! Success may whisk a few souls from low-born to high-born in one generation but there are others descending even faster in the goods lift. From Fred the Shred to Fred the Dunderhead, pocketer of an absurdly large pension, king of the credit crunchers, the man who helped to wreck Edinburgh's standing as a financial centre. I'll bet his local tradesmen aren't so keen to secure his custom nowadays. The drinks party invitations must have dried up like a Somali bore hole. And then came his shunning by the Royal and Ancient golf club in St Andrews, whose membership is much coveted. What a ridiculous footnote, said some. I thought it was reassuring. The class system is quicker to drop people than it is to take them up and that is how it should be. Salt on the cut. A painful but necessary corrective. Sir Fred Goodwin may, for the moment, be keeping his fat pension but he has lost the good opinion of his countrymen and I bet that rejection by the Royal and Ancient hurt him as much as the disappearance of various noughts from his personal bank account.

Members of the babyboom elite affect to deplore privilege. This does not stop them leaping on petty advantage. Any chance of an airline upgrade? Any possibility my daughter could come and do some work experience at your advertising agency? This is the generation that sets such store by the ability to reserve a table at the (actually not terribly good) Ivy restaurant yet deplores the Athenaeum club in Pall Mall as unacceptably elitist. The people at the Athenaeum actually tend to be a lot more friendly.

Disgrace mechanisms are important. A privileged person should know that if he does a Brocket or an Archer or a Goodwin he will go sliding down the razor blade towards V for Vulgar, using his balls for brakes. Unlikeable as the political correctness martinets are, it is rather admirable the way they have contrived to impart such professional disgrace to anyone who whispers a racist or sexist or homophobic sentiment. The sky falls in. Carol Thatcher found this when she made a loose remark about a black tennis player in what she thought was a private conversation. Derek Walcott fell out of the contest to be Oxford Poetry Professor after questions about his attitude to women. Barack Obama, of all people, had trouble with the disabled lobby after a light-hearted comment about the Paralympics. All three cases were ludicrously overblown yet the machinery of disgrace was impressive. Would that we had it to police social attitudes to courtesy and discipline.

After all, what is disapproval if not a form of 'snobbery'?

Polly's Pepper

There is no collective in Britain more hand-wringingly egalitarian than the *Guardian* newspaper. Its editorial conferences are a parade in sensitivity. So keen are this centre-Left paper's managers to be accessible – to live their thesis that every voice is valid – that they throw open the morning news meeting to all their journalists. Other papers limit conferences to a handful of power-bangers. Not the *Guardian*. In the words of those under-recognised social democrats, the three musketeers, 'tis one for all and all for one.

At the centre of this chin-stroking throng sits the bespectacled figure of the editor, Alan Rusbridger, an owlish soul of donnish mien and crumpled suits. If Alan seldom remembers to brush his hair it is only because he is too busy thinking, ruminating on life's injustices, intellectualising the thuggishness of the proletariat. Busy Alan, in his few spare hours a delicate pianist and supportive friend of multi-millionare tax loophole artist Lord Myners, is open to everyone's view, from the scurviest diary hack to the dimmest fashion writer. Everyone is allowed to contribute. No opinion, unless by some very slim chance it be snortingly right-wing, is subjected to the chastening acid of mockery. No! Not at the *Guardian*.

Ancient Greece would have struggled to match the pooled perspicacity, the earnest striving of this prune-faced gathering. To one corner of the room perches high-born Polly Toynbee, crusader against private schools, champion of the state, and Tuscan property tycoon. In another corner languishes suave Seumas Milne, the Che Guevara of Chelsea, himself patrician – Old Wykehamist son of a BBC director-general – and yet unyielding in his devotion to classlessness. Comrade Seumas will not rest in sinew and bone until every last seam of privilege has been quarried and cast from British soil.

If only Rembrandt were still with us to capture the scene, this symposium of eager frowns raised towards the central Solomon with his unkempt barnet and chewed Biro. All hail the saintly Rusbridger and his crew. And to a point I mean it. There *is* something wonderful about these well-meaning ninnies' desire to 'balance injustice'. It chimes with much Christian teaching. On first inspection it is more admirable than selfish libertarianism. It's just a pity that by rejecting rank, by denying the inevitability of a hierarchy of values, they are destroying the surest means by which poorer people can climb from the abyss.

Until Monsanto scientists have recrafted our DNA and turned us into identical, straight cucumbers, humans will separate into categories like so many blobs of mercury, no matter how much the high-born Mary Louisa Toynbee jumps up and down in her booties and demands sovietised homogeneity. The difference between humans and mercury is that we can move of our own volition from one blob to another. That much-deplored thing called class offers us a virtuous direction of travel. That, in turn, sets communal values which can create a more civilised, happy society for everyone. Class is an instrument of progressive civic values. Far from preventing social mobility, it encourages it. Polly and her people should positively embrace class, and not just the Tuscan villas part of it.

One of the tragi-comic paradoxes of our time is that no newspaper has done more to legitimise the bad language – the horrid, decivilising dirtiness – heard in our society than this Torah of tolerance, the *Guardian*. Profanities pollute twenty-first-century Britain. They elbow their way into our conversations, tarnishing the flavour of national life as surely as a tang of Silver Dip on a forkful of scrambled egg. Foul language demeans us all. It leaves a nasty taste. It violates us, drags those in its orbit down to the lowest level and creates an atmosphere in which physical violence is the next step.

We expect rough language on a building site. We might even expect it (and indeed find it) in the newsroom of a mid-market newspaper where tempers fray towards the deadline hour. And yet here we find it being promoted publicly by a newspaper which claims to be written by and for intelligent people with a conscience, a paper of progressive politics, a paper which appeals to teachers and social workers and organic mushroom pickers in Cardiganshire.

It would be absurd to suggest that no one swore before, say, 1963. I bet even Enid Blyton let rip with the occasional cuss. But before the mid-1960s people didn't do it so much and they were certainly not rewarded for it with millions of pounds of public money, as has been the case with Jonathan Ross. The newspaper most supportive of Ross during his expletive-spattered career on the publicly funded airwaves? The *Guardian*.

This same *Guardian* (and to a smaller extent the *Independent*, whose buccaneering editor swears like a lance-bombardier) has no time for the asterisks used by family newspapers to indicate swearing. It revels in ribaldries, printing them with abandon. Its soignée, educated columnists seem to take their cue from those poor souls you sometimes see walking down the street, swinging their arms and hurling impieties at the four winds. These writers want to be as foul-mouthed as hoi polloi. They think swearing is pleb-exotic.

They are obsessed with discussing sex, too. Not long ago one *Guardian* writer, Charlie Brooker, dwelt in his column on a new homosexual term, 'docking'. It involved ... well, let us not repeat Brooker's description, save to say that he accompanied this anatomically detailed passage with a self-hurrah about how only the *Guardian* would give you such information. This same Brooker is regularly lauded as a maestro of the columnar art and even won a prize at the 2009 British Press Awards. He is quite the most modish creature going. He is thought to be 'edgy' (an approving euphemism for base).

Why do the men and women in our society's leading positions prostrate themselves before the goblin of vulgarity? This is more than a mere quest for sales. There is something deeper-rooted at work, something twisted, approval-seeking. We British are often accused of having a class obsession but today we are obsessed with appearing bog-standard class rather than hoity-toity privileged. We need not pretend that, as adults, we never misbehave. Of course we do. Some of us might even gossip, in private, about the meaning of terms such as Mr Brooker's 'docking'. But to do so in one-to-one conversation is different to slapping it down in print on the pages of a newspaper whose whole identity is about the well-being of society.

Things are not much better on the West End stage. *Priscilla Queen of the Desert* is a mainstream musical in which, at one point, a gay character describes the ability of one of his boyfriends to wrap a gingernut biscuit inside his foreskin. The night I went to *Priscilla*, the majority of theatregoers (the house included children) seemed stunned by the bad taste. Was this truly family entertainment? Or was it a conscious, political attempt to lower our expectations of decency? This is one of the tactics of bog-standardisation. It blunts the nation's susceptibility to shock.

The *Guardian*, a great newspaper in numerous ways, is regarded by workers at the BBC and throughout the public sector as something akin to holy writ. It is such a staple of life for many of our administrators that it acquires greater influence than might be expected from a publication with such a modest circulation. Silly Charlie Brooker trashes any idea of self-censorship in public life. When the lewd can be so easily bandied about, by what check can we hope to improve the racist, capital-punishment-supporting, materialistic, carbon-wasting rabble? Where is the idea of a shared decency? *Guardian* journalists are enthusiasts for citizenship studies in our schools. Where is the citizenship in a newspaper and in state-subsidised television stations whose commissioning editors encourage bad language? Less educated mortals hear it being used on terrestrial television and think, well, if it's on the BBC it must be acceptable. They need not think 'swearing is for yobboes' or 'swearing will stop you being promoted'. The very notion of a yobbo and of low class becomes elusive. That Jonathan Ross makes a fortune and *he* swears. Well, let's follow suit and flick two fingers at the frightened young mothers who ask us to pipe down when we shout the word in the vicinity of their toddlers.

This problem arises because leading members of the Left are uncomfortable viewing themselves as leaders. Alan Rusbridger and Polly Toynbee and Seumas Milne probably think pretty mightily of themselves. They would be right to do so, because they are fine journalists. But it is time they publicly acknowledged that they are an elite. That brings responsibility, not just in paying a higher rate of income tax but also in behaviour.

Earthy language is sometimes called 'Anglo-Saxon' and there are blue jokes in English literature as early as Chaucer. What is different today is the scale and brazenness. Profanities are heard everywhere. BBC executives have pushed the penny an eighth of an inch at a time, doing so with childish giggling. A twerp called Simon Shaps, former director of television at ITV, has called the use of the F word on television 'a small victory for free speech against the forces of darkness and repression'. A victory for ignorance and ineloquence, more like, a victory for gruntfuttocking dumbers-down and bottom-feeding ratings tarts who ignore the brutalising impact their programmes have had on our society.

Let us pause a moment to give this Shaps a Chinese burn. Writing in the *Independent*, he rejoiced in the rise of bad language on telly and thought that this showed television had 'caught up with the twenty-first century, particularly the world inhabited by a younger generation'. Oh no, not another ageing groover desperate to keep in with spotty youth. Far from television 'catching up' with youth slang, it has normalised it, desensitising the rest of us so that we no longer see any point in complaining. Having written a long paean to the power of shock, Mr Shaps closed his article by saying that the word 'golliwog' on television had 'no possible defence' because it was 'small-minded and profoundly out of touch'. Come, come, Shaps. What happened to your objection to 'repression'? What happened to your delight in words simply for their power to cause 'shock'?

What we have with the likes of this low-thoughted macaroon is linguistic mob rule, a corrupting addiction to the worst society has to offer rather than its best, simply so that he and his sticky-fingered friends can make more money from their broadcasts. We should no more allow men like Simon Shaps to run our television stations than we would allow Dennis Nilsen to run a Cub Scout pack in Amersham.

Some of the oddest areas have been hijacked by profanity. Television cookery shows are now worse than salty. One had the F word 232 times in two hours. Gordon Ramsay can barely chop a spring onion without blaspheming. Perhaps it is a subconscious metaphor about 'letting off steam' in a hot kitchen, but I doubt it. It is more likely a blatant anti-class ramp, an attempt to 'democratise' cooking and make it raucous rather than refined. I once interviewed Ramsay and found him less a tiger than a somnolent kitten. Away from the television camera he was thoughtful, benevolent, polite. So why must we have all this Ramsayish bragging in public, all this machismo and malice? Why must we have these lurid tales about his boyhood being rough? Why the rudeness about that Australian television presenter he called a porker? Why must we have this image of the cook on a rolling boil, some sort of larder terrorist, the pantry oik whose language could curdle a béchamel sauce? Calm down, Gordon. Civilise yourself. Bring yourself off this silly simmer. The anger is as confected as one of your sticky little *petits-fours*. Mind you, the mateying-down of cookery has not stopped Ramsay charging astronomical sums at his restaurants. They are among the most *recherché* establishments in London and I dare say that if you entered one and swore at the maître d' you would be asked to leave. Quite right, too.

Social sanction is the way to stop verbal brutality. It is time our brightest fiftysomethings grew out of their jeans and silly haircuts and accepted the duty of leadership. It is time they stopped fannying around with feeble talk about the 'validity' of inferior habits and behaviours. We need to become *more* judgemental, not less.

Terrestrial broadcasters should not only censor profanities. They should also, except in rare cases, ban the bleeped passage of dialogue. Too often the bleeped word is followed by a burst of laughter from a studio audience. Bleeping reinforces the idea that swearing – even if we have not heard the exact word – is funny. It ain't.

Call Me Tony

When Tony Blair entered 10 Downing Street in 1997 he instructed the Cabinet to 'call me Tony'. Gushy commentators praised Mr Blair for relaxing the code of business at the top of public life. It was such a change from the formality of old, from the 'yes, Prime Minister' days when office holders were addressed by their title. First-name terms: how democratic!

How bogus, more like. Familiarity was not matched by equality of clout. Mr Blair ignored his ministers whether they called him Tony or not. The only person who addressed him by his surname was George W. Bush, who shouted 'Yo, Blair!' at a summit, hailing our Prime Minister as an Edwardian clubman might summon the sherry waiter.

In his pomp Mr Blair was feared by colleagues almost as much as starchy Margaret Thatcher, who could make ministers dampen their smalls simply by lifting one of her kirby-grip eyebrows. Yet Prime Minister Blair wished to be thought youthful, unstuffy, approachable. For centuries it was the British way to observe a distinction between individuals and the offices they held. Now it was discarded. Secretaries of State who should have had regard for national and departmental interests were lured into a flattering coterie. The use of Christian names only made it more awkward to disagree with the vainglorious, cufflinked popinjay in No. 10. The wasteful Millennium Dome was opposed by most members of the Cabinet yet ministers rolled over on being told, by John Prescott, that 'Tony' wanted it. First-name terms rusted the self-respect of the Cabinet. Its members started seeing things not as Government decisions but as something more personal.

Amateur farmers – the Tom and Barbara Goods of this world – are always advised not to give their piglets names because they will find it harder to send them to the slaughterhouse when they think of them as 'Matilda' or 'Fluffy'. The same emotional sterility should apply among colleagues in public life. Propriety with titles makes it easier to send a counterpart's bad policy to the knacker's yard. Formality is a fire-break against corruption. In so many areas of work we have lost that sensible stiffness because we are terrified of sounding snooty.

When former army officer Iain Duncan Smith was Leader of the Conservative Party he was admitted to Downing Street for Privy Council briefings with the Prime Minister. Maybe it was his background in the armed forces or maybe it was his natural respect for the office of Prime Minister, but the gentlemanly Duncan Smith addressed Mr Blair as 'sir'. Given that some of the briefings were about the likelihood of war against Iraq, a little formality was not out of place. 'Sir' might have reminded Mr Blair – a man with an all too slovenly view of the traditions of high office – that he was taking decisions of a momentous nature. Although those meetings were confidential, newspapers somehow learned that Blair aides thought it hilarious that the Tory leader was calling the PM 'sir'. Readers were told that this only showed how out of touch the Tory leader was. What a twerp IDS must be to show such respect (so ran the tenor of the articles). With hindsight we can wish that Mr Duncan Smith had used different epithets. 'Little runt' or 'treacherous fox' or 'stool-pigeon of American imperialism' might have done, might they not? What we should not do, though, is mock IDS's respect for the gradations of office. He had the right idea.

The Left has long misunderstood equality in this sense. It suspected that the Right was too hidebound by respect for command (fair point in some ways), but it failed to see that authority can be the ally of personal liberty. Former Commons Speaker Michael Martin, in declining to wear the flowing robes and wig of his male predecessors, thought he was showing how egalitarian he was. All he was doing was denuding his office of its proper distance from the world – a distance which made the Speakership better respected. A Speaker who acts like an Olympian deity, spurning the fellowship of other MPs, is more likely to be seen as an unbiased adjudicator and protector of the individual. Mr Martin lolled around in his Chair, chatted to Labour MPs and winked at friends. The only time he showed an appreciation for status was if he thought his own dignity had been dented by, say, a patrician Tory. Down he came like a ton of haggis meat, yelling: 'Dooon't you tell me how to do mah job!'

Defending formality is not a modish pursuit. One risks being called a fogey. All right, fair cop, guv. Let your author admit to holding old-fashioned views on many matters and to living, in rural Herefordshire, in a Britain which is disappearing as fast as a mermaid's kneecaps. I read books. I write letters with a fountain pen. I polish my shoes. I attend church and like singing the 'Te Deum'. I love my wife and, at the time of writing, she seems to have a reasonably benign view of me. I follow this way of life not to burnish my chances of making it to St Peter's gates. I do so because such routines make me happy, because I was taught to do so by my parents and because

I want to introduce my children to the same morale-boosting ways. I do these things because they tie in with a tested idea of what is good for one, an idea of self-improvement – in short, of 'getting ahead'. Tradition is actually rather a forward-looking proposition. It's a good bet for the future.

The dismissal of such views simply on some charge of cultural archaism is madness. That kneejerk antipathy to old ways – the motive that made Tony Blair order ministers to 'call me Tony' – has brought us to the sorry, boggy standard of Britain today.

The Politics of Names

Mononyms used to be rare. There was a 1930s jazz singer called Hutch (my late grandmother liked him). There was Coco the clown. Long before that there was the prophet known simply as Moses. These days mononymed chancers are more numerous: Duffy, Pink, Lulu (pop star), Lula (Brazilian president), Twiggy, Posh, Cher. An Irish musician called Paul Hewson would not have become quite such a Pied Piper had he not renamed himself Bono. Because he has that mononym he is held to have some special power and the world's teeming billions pause before his pink-spectacled platitudes about sharing wealth.

Would we have swallowed quite so much claptrap from Sting if he had used publicly his real name of Gordon Sumner? Brazilian footballers Pele and Kaka and Ronaldinho somehow gain in stature by having only the one moniker. Such is the strange politics of names. By demanding to be known just by one name these people are trying to say, 'I am so well known, so loved by the people, that I do not need a surname.' They think they are being democratic but their monomania may have more to do with arrogance. Our little friend Bono bangs on about poverty in Africa yet he himself is as hungry a capitalist as the next man, running a large, carnivorous concern. Unlike the poor of the sub-equatorial continent, there are no flies on businessman

Bono. He is actually rather better at making money (and using shrewd tax advisers) than he is at holding the note on a high A. And yet this bore lectures the modestly paid about their duty to give to the poor. The BBC laps him up. Yes, equality was a good career choice for Bono. Other people's poverty has been the making of him.

To call someone 'Mr' is the conversational equivalent of using a Corby trouser press – incorrigibly untrendy. Even to use surnames is regarded as slightly infra dig. Forenames, as with Tony Blair and his Cabinet, are bandied about in the empty belief that they can give officialdom a friendly face. Parents are encouraged to address their children's schoolteachers by their first names – not 'Miss Pettigrew' but 'Becky', say. Miss Pettigrew, in turn, will address them not as 'Mr and Mrs Wright' but as 'Mike and Angie'. This makes it harder to exact professional standards from the school. It makes it harder to complain about 'Becky' if she is a useless teacher. Emasculated by familiarity, parents are at a disadvantage. They may want to scream at Miss Pettigrew because they think her trendy teaching methods are claptrap, a dumbed-down con, but because she insists on being called 'Becky' they dare not upset the woman. Teachers today consider themselves to be equal in rank to the parents they are meant to serve. They do not want to be seen in the role of employee because that would reduce their power.

An official trip to India in early 2009 by the Foreign Secretary, David Miliband, went awry thanks to this new British laxness with names. Mr Miliband made a speech in which he referred to India's venerable Foreign Minister, Pranab Mukherjee, by his first name. The 73-year-old Mr Mukherjee, thoroughly unchuffed by the whippersnapper's cheek, did not return the compliment. He preferred to address Mr Miliband pointedly as 'Excellency'. He did not mean it – only a man on magic mushrooms could truly think Mr Miliband was excellent – but the term 'Excellency' is an honorific, redolent of rank and attendant respect. Such attitudes are strikingly out of fashion among Britain's twenty-first-century elite. How depressing that post-colonial India is now more alive to the notions of command and dignity of office than its former colonial ruler. An Indian official was later quoted as referring to Mr Miliband witheringly as 'a young man'. There is certainly something jejune in the way London's ruling crowd refuses to dress up, linguistically, to the occasion.

Former Home Secretary Jacqui Smith also learned how dangerous it was to dispense with formality when she was caught referring to Assistant Commissioner Robert Quick of New Scotland Yard as 'Bob'. This led to Copper Quick being labelled the Home Secretary's 'favourite policeman'. At the time he was caught up in the controversy of the arrest of Damian Green, a Conservative frontbench MP. Should a friend of the Home Secretary really be feeling the collar of one of her political opponents? Not ideal, is it? The result was damage to the reputation of Miss Smith and a weakening of any case against suspect Green. Had she only referred to him, properly, as 'Mr Quick' or 'the Assistant Commissioner', there might have been no such trouble. But she thought official titles stuffy. Mr Quick later lost his job after mistakenly enabling long-lens photographers to snap a secret document in Downing Street. Miss Smith, with her expenses problems, did not last much longer.

Public life needs top dogs. It ceases to function if those elected to its most senior positions decline to conduct themselves in a rarefied manner. The nature of positions such as the Speakership is to be non-equal. Those who reach positions of such responsibility must put away childish things. They must become tools of duty, leading the community in order to strengthen it. A Speaker must, like a monk or nun, surrender to a life of cloistered remoteness. That may be out of keeping with the 'call me Tony' approach of the egalitarian age. Tough. In the long run it is more equal because the body politic – the legal and electoral circuit board which sustains our rights – will be better served.

Chris Mullin MP, in his diaries, describes energy-sapping battles he had about his office when he was junior Minister for International Aid. A new departmental building was planned and the Permanent Secretary, Sir John Vereker, apparently wanted the large office reserved for Mr Mullin. Sir John was said to have waged a canny campaign and Minister Mullin said he eventually agreed that Sir John could have the large office because he, Mullin, was not interested in 'status'. In some ways we can admire Mr Mullin's distaste for personal glory. Might the civil service not have been deservedly put in its place, however, if Sir John had been squashed? Status for personal comfort is silly but status as a symbol of the seniority of the politically accountable minister over the unelected official is worth having. Mr Mullin should have told Sir John that he was exceeding his proper station.

New Labour MPs who entered Parliament in 1997 were slow to appreciate the formal modes of debate. Commons questions had to be put in the third person rather than the second person singular. Such conventions may seem fusty, but the third-person rule prevents debate becoming too personal and reminds the minister of his or her office. This notion of 'speaking through the Chair' is a useful civiliser of Parliament. Without it the Commons might unravel to the point MPs engaged in fisticuffs (as happens in the South Korean assembly, where they could do with Harry Carpenter to present 'Yesterday in Parliament'). David Cameron has occasionally used the second person singular when attacking his opponent at Prime Minister's Questions. The first couple of times it was new and sharp. Now it sounds cheap.

Similarly, there is a pecking order in Parliament, although it is little understood outside the Palace of Westminster. Cabinet ministers become Privy Counsellors and may then call themselves 'Rt Hon.' for life. Oh, they love it. You can almost hear them purr when they are addressed as 'the Rt Hon. Member'. Sheer egotism on one level, yet on a more elevated plane it is society's way of showing these politicians that the country now has certain expectations of them. God knows, we could do with some better behaviour from our political leaders. Restoring the esteem of titles might be an idea. Recent Cabinet ministers have tried to dilute their titles. Tony Blair and his wheezing Stavros, Lord Falconer, tried to do down the grandeur of the Lord High Chancellorship. They partly failed, thank goodness. Let us pin these people up against the bicycle shed wall in future and say, 'Now look here, you've been given a fancy title, let's see you earn it by behaving like proper leaders.'

Earlier this year, officials at the European Parliament made horses of themselves by urging the Brussels bureaucracy not to use the words 'Miss' or 'Mrs' or their equivalents in other languages. Instead they should use 'gender-neutral' language – i.e. a linguistic version of equality. Words such as 'waitress', 'salesman' and 'cinema usherette' were to be frowned on owing to their 'sexist' bent. Instead of 'sportsman', the word 'athlete' was to be used. Ditto 'political leader' for 'statesman', 'artificial' for 'man-made' and so forth. God help us. Do they really imagine that anyone is truly upset by such language? The *Guardian* in its obituary of the Italian film producer Carlo Ponti, wrote that he was 'a man with a good eye for pretty actors': a ludicrously strict adherence to its style guide – couldn't it just have simply used 'actresses'? – that ended up offending his grieving family. As for those replacement words, how boring they are. Blandness Torpor. It may sound like a village in Dorset but it is the upshot of egalitarian excess.

Formality bestows order. Order, in turn, allows everyone to be heard. Is that not a more equal way of going about things?

Don't Kick the Bucket Woman

Social climbing, much sneered at by class warriors, means people are trying to make the most of themselves. Good for Ann Gloag, once a burns-unit nurse, now owner of two castles having made a fortune with the Stagecoach bus company. She has earned the right to stride her battlements. Let us cheer the mother of Kate Middleton for working hard and ascending the social Himalayas. Once an air stewardess, she is now a county mum whose daughter is stepping out with the son of the heir to the throne. Soupier-minded Hoorays who attach themselves to the royal circle reportedly mock Mrs Middleton by calling her 'Doors to Manual'. They should be grounded.

Personally I would not care to have a butler clogging up the house, but some people's taste runs to that sort of thing. We can tease Shaun Woodward MP for keeping hot and cold running servants at his various houses but if he wants to boost the employment market, long may he be at liberty to do so. It is his money (or, to be more accurate, his wife's money). The same must be true of that strutty little bantam Lord Sugar, now set for the peerage. After a meeting at Downing Street, business swami Alan was photographed trotting down to his Rolls-Royce motor car. His gait was that of a Badminton horse in the dressage arena. The Roller's personalised number plate may be as naff as a silver shellsuit but there are plenty of better reasons for recoiling from Milord Sugar (e.g. his litigiousness).

We Brits have long tickled social climbers. An early example was George and Weedon Grossmith's *Diary of a Nobody*, gently satirising the stiff-collared clerical class with a taste for holidays in Broadstairs. More recently there has been Hyacinth Bucket in the television series *Keeping Up Appearances*. Patricia Routledge plays suburban housewife Hyacinth, a queen of pretensions who pronounces her surname 'Bouquet'. The opening credits show her laying out the placements for a dinner party. She is in the grip of genteel propriety, be it presenting a front to the vicar or insisting that her son Sheridan is a go-getter with marital prospects. In fact he is a wastrel, more likely to be found sniffing amyl nitrates at a gay pub. Another dark secret of Hyacinth's life is that her sister lives on a rough estate with husband Onslow, a burpy slob in bulging string vest. Hyacinth is torn by their failure to maintain standards. Every time she visits them a dog barks from the inside of an abandoned car. Every time Hyacinth ends up in the hedge, clutching her throat in fright.

The laughter in *Keeping Up Appearances* is directed at Hyacinth for refusing to acknowledge where she comes from. Yet we surely also admire her for trying to make the best of herself. Hyacinth Bucket is an example to us, a productive member of society rather than a benefit sponger, a maintainer of standards of sobriety rather than the drunken aggro of the world she has escaped.

The programme was conceived in the early 1990s. Today's middle classes have become so timid that they no longer bother to 'keep up appearances'. Most of them try, instead, to keep appearances down. They do not bother to support the church, as Hyacinth does. How many women wear a hat? If visiting slothful relations they take round a few tinnies of supermarket bitter to watch the footy rather than trying to tell them to mend their ways. Today we drop to the lower level rather than rising to the higher.

At whose house would you rather stay the night – Hyacinth's or her sister's? So why is our popular culture so skewed to the Onslows of this world?

Vivat Hyacinth.

Awright, Mate?

here we sat on the Thomson Holidays coach at Innsbruck
airport, feeling pretty good about life – or as good as it is
possible to feel on a coach. It was the start of a week's skiing in
Austria, an expensive but enjoyable way to spend the New Year.
We were splurging some of our earnings on a holiday. And why
not? One of the pleasures of a holiday or a new car or an evening
at a restaurant is the knowledge that you are using your own
money. Extravagance is fun. It is a reward after toil. There
should be nothing wrong in looking forward to being treated as
a valued customer.

On to our bus clambered a young, sloppily dressed woman.
She had one of those jaunty names, Niki or Jen or something like
that. She seized the in-bus microphone and blew into it so that it
made a loud noise. 'Hi, guys,' she said. Eurrrrgh. Guys. Not one
of the paying clients on the bus was younger than she was, yet we
were being hailed as 'guys' who deserved only a sub-American
'hi' rather than a 'how do you do?' Why could we not be greeted
as 'ladies and gentlemen'? Even a plain 'good morning, all' – I
suppose a Dixon of Dock Green salute would have been too
much to expect – would have been preferable. This woman was
our travel rep. She owed her job to our custom. By blowing hard
into that microphone, making it pop, she had already

demonstrated amateurishness and a tin ear for courtesy. Now she was treating us like equals.

'Ladies and gentlemen' is considered by some to be hierarchical. Lefties hate the phrase. To them it smacks of the provincial toastmaster or the windbag at a Conservative Party fundraiser. The 'hi', similarly, was indicative of egalitarian, anti-snobbish terror. 'Hi' is trying to establish itself as the norm for greetings, particularly in emails. Its enthusiasts feel that it is somehow more democratic and accessible, even when they have no right to assume parity with the people they are addressing. Why should customers who have paid several thousand pounds to go skiing be subjected to this mateyness? They might prefer to be addressed with respect. The travel entrepreneur who starts an upmarket company named 'We'll Call You "Sir"' could be on to a winner.

The idea that such informality is somehow North American is mistaken. Yes, 'hi' is a US salutation, but an American travel rep would greet clients with elaborate politeness. American shop assistants thank you as 'sir' or 'ma'am' – and it sounds natural, not claggy. Americans use these terms the way the French happily use 'Monsieur' and 'Madame/Mademoiselle' and the Spanish use 'Señor' and 'Señora/Señorita'. Modern Brit counterparts find it demeaning to extend such courtesies. From time to time I buy a newspaper at the draughty branch of WH Smith at a West Country railway station. It is often manned by a casual man of about thirty, pale-faced with darkish, greasy hair. He has the air of an unsuccessful Giles Coren. When I buy my newspaper he, almost without fail, addresses me languidly as 'mate' – even, one particularly shuddersome day, as 'buddy boy'. He does this not because he recognises me after all these years of custom, nor does he do it to be friendly. He does it in a tone of bland contempt, as though eager to establish himself as my equal – which he is not. In civilian life he may or may not be my social superior, but while he is behind that counter, serving me, he is the merchant and I am the customer. Time to cough up some respect, buddy boy.

Mateyness is everywhere. Radio presenters chat vapidly with the weather forecaster or the road traffic reports person, convinced that their witterings are of interest. They applaud one another for doing the jobs for which we (more often than not) are paying them – 'thank you for that weather forecast, Liam, terrific'. This chumminess becomes infectious. Call centre staff are so programmed to speak to customers by their Christian names that it quite throws them when you try to use your surname.

Nevil Shute's novel *Ordeal* imagines a military attack on the south of England. The central character, Corbett, visits a doctor. The doctor is godfather to one of Corbett's children. There the two friends find themselves, in terrible peril while their home town is being bombed to near-destruction, yet they fastidiously address each other by their surnames. Even in such a moment of civic danger their social training endures. It helps them to keep control of their panic. Manners are like the bones of a trout. Although individually delicate, they provide a frame which prevents the structure flopping and flubbing like a plastic bag filled with sludge. To address a close friend nowadays by his surname would be impractical. But is there not some truth in the thought that over-familiarity is lax, insincere and weakens the stoicism for which our country was once celebrated?

Crackle and Slop

One of the boggier blights on British life is the railway announcement. These come in two forms. There is the station platform announcement, a patchwork of metallic sounds barely recognisable as human. Then there is the carriage intercom infomercial, a strange mixture of corporate-speak, hard sell and rampaging egomania, all apparently delivered through a sock.

The platform announcements are so important that they can no longer be entrusted to human beings. First you hear that hellish *bing bong* – insistent, high, tinny. It jabs the eardrums, more painful with each rendition. Grown adults brace themselves and briefly contemplate stabbing themselves with the station canteen's knives until they remember that they are plastic and will only shatter into tiny white shards. And now, horror, comes the blast of computerised, chopped-up words, a composite of dead-fish information. The railway (sorry, 'train operating company') has paid some woman with flat vowels to record a spread of words and phrases such as 'train', 'platform', 'is now arriving', 'first-class accommodation at the front of the train' and a specially chirrupy 'we apologise for this delay'. These words and phrases, pasted together like a police photo-fit crime suspect picture, are then broadcast according to requirements. It is plain that they have been programmed by some centralised announcements machine, probably two counties away. They talk about 'the train now approaching platform three' even though no train can be seen for half a mile. Or perhaps there is already a train standing at platform three. Whatever, the announcement is frequently a nonsense. On they continue, for ages, running through the names of the various destinations, rendering your mobile telephone call impossible. Syllables are joined together in a vocal equivalent of badly cut jigsaw puzzle pieces. In an announcement that 'the next train to arrive at platform two will be the 10.46 for London Paddington', the word 'two' will shoot out early, darting in so fast that it is almost lost in the end of 'platform'. The words 'London Paddington' (I wish they'd just say 'London') will also sound different – more jagged – making it obvious that this is a manufactured announcement. The apologies could scarcely sound less genuine. Computer says sorry for making such a balls-up of your journey? Great. That's really sincere. Meanwhile, the only official-looking bod on the platform is a mildewed halfwit in a yellow jacket, holding a walkie talkie which he cannot hear owing to the platform announcement.

It wasn't always like this. At Swindon, I remember that the platform announcements used to be made by a man with a faint Wiltshire burr to his voice. His tone was deep and clear. He was a model of clarity and you had more faith in his announcements because he was so obviously just a door or so away, there at the station. With the modern platform announcements there is no sense of the voice actually belonging to the station reality. It might as well be – and for all we know, is – a message pinged down the line from head office. Why couldn't they leave the old announcer in his place? Because he might become too popular and that might make it harder for the corporate profit maniacs to sack him if they needed to shave costs to meet some bonus payout for the railway's directors.

The on-board announcements are no better. These tend to be made by the guard (sorry, 'train manager') or by the canteen wallah ('chief steward'). Fluent or even passable English is not, apparently, a requirement. It is common for the Tannoy to have a loose connection so that only part of each sentence is audible. 'This is the fnarrr crccccc flllfff hyfcot Parkway, Reading and London Paddincrfffff.' Oh, they love it. The power! Microphone diarrhoea ensues, the person in charge of the PA system burbling away at length before and after every 'station stop' ('stop', we used to call them). The egalitarian assumption by these people and the bosses who train them is that the majority of passengers are mentally subnormal. Fair point in some ways. We must be pretty naïve to pay so much money to travel on such horrible trains, but that is a different debate. So dumbed-down is the railway announcer's approach that we have to be told, each time the train draws out of a station, the whereabouts of the caff, the availability of 'freshly made sangwiches and hot and cold beverages', the fact that smoking is forbidden, the existence of quiet carriages – WELL SHUT UP, THEN – and the desirability of having tickets ready for inspection when the ticket inspector comes through the train. We know! Leave us in peace!

Waiting Game

Any tramp who found a £50 note, tidied himself up and walked in to the dining room of the Connaught to order breakfast would expect to be treated well by the maître d' – and no doubt he would be. Good service demands respect for the customer. One of the better military customs involves officers serving their mess waiters once a year. The same thing happens at our children's school, where the headmaster and his staff serve the annual feast just before the end of the Christmas term. A more elevated example of this respect and humility was of Christ washing the feet of his followers – a symbolic act which the Church of England has reintroduced, clergy washing the feet of congregants during Holy Week. By placing ourselves in the position of humble servant we show that we have not become so arrogant that we expect always to be pampered. It is a guard against egomania.

Pleasure in the art of service has slipped in Britain. Service in restaurants and bars is often amateurish and surly. This is as sure an indicator of malaise as a coal mine's canary starting to tie a gas mask to its lower beak. Waiters in countries less paranoid about egalitarianism tend to be happier in their lot. They willingly wear uniform and yield to the convention that the customer is never wrong. Look at the waiters on the streets of Paris or Barcelona. They swagger. They swing their hips and balance trays on one flat palm. They pinch children's cheeks and flirt with the ladies. They are certain of their station in life, accept it, enjoy its showier possibilities and bring joy to others around them.

Bad service makes customers peevish and robs employees of pride in their jobs. To say so is not snooty. It is a simple business truth. The other side of the deal is that customers should show understanding to the waiter. You can tell a great deal about someone's character from the way he or she treats waiters. Americans (particularly New Yorkers) sometimes whinge at waiters in nasty, nasal voices. This is one of the worst things about the US. We are catching the disease here. A habit has spread of customers telling waiters, 'I'll get the roast beef' when they in fact mean 'I would like some roast beef, please'. The verb 'get' is always best avoided but never more so than when talking to restaurant staff.

Simlarly, anyone who takes the 'don't you know who I am?' approach is, pretty clearly, an ass. Mary Martin, wife of the former Speaker, reportedly used the 'don't you know who I am?' gambit when she was stopped at the entrance to the Palace of Westminster and asked to show her security pass. One newspaper suggested that Mrs Martin, reared in a poor family in Glasgow, became quite the Restoration comedy lady when pressed for her credentials. Ledley King, a Tottenham Hotspur and England footballer, allegedly asked bouncers 'don't you know who I am?' when denied entrance to the Punk nightclub, central London, in May 2009. A fight ensued. Didn't they know who Ledley was? They certainly did when the newspapers jumped on the story and reported that he was helping police with their inquiries. And then there was the case of Gurbux Singh, former head of the Commission for Racial

Equality, who had a boozy argument with police at Lord's cricket ground. 'Do you know who I am?' demanded Mr Singh. 'I know Blair. I'll have your job.' He was referring to Ian Blair, then a senior Metropolitan Police officer. Should a Pooh-Bah of the equality industry not have remembered that we are all equal in the eyes of the law and that the question 'do you know who I am?' is celebrity snobbery at its worst?

Ah, but this is modern Britain. You do not, surely, expect the crack troops of egalitarianism to forgo the privileges of office. Come, come!

Not to Knight, Thank You

Class paranoia is so rampant that public figures honoured by the Queen sometimes hesitate to use their titles in case that makes them sound too upper-class. Media grandees are particularly guilty of this. Take the case of Sir Simon Jenkins, former editor of *The Times* and the *Evening Standard*, now columnist for the *Guardian* and chairman of the National Trust. Sir Simon is a superb writer and a civilised man, imbued with a sense of public service. And yet he dislikes being addressed as a knight of the realm. If you call him 'Sir Simon' he adopts a pained expression, like a man who has just seen his train pull out of the platform without him.

The same is true of my old editor Sir Max Hastings. Twenty years ago many of us at the *Daily Telegraph* would have marched across the Sahara for editor Max. God, he was difficult. Had the bark of a sealion. Stomped about the office like a Falklands soldier yomping to Port Stanley and would write such terrifying memos that his secretary, Rachel, delivered them as though they were live hand grenades. She would place them gingerly on your desk with an apology and then reverse away, her gaze pitying. Yet Max was a tremendously exciting, demanding boss. He defended his hacks from litigious fraudsters and sometimes those memos could include bombastic words of praise. He went on to edit the *Evening*

Standard, did a stint in charge of the Campaign to Protect Rural England, made some high-quality documentaries and has written excellent history books. He, like Sir Simon Jenkins, deserved his knighthood. Yet he will not have the 'Sir' used in his journalistic by-line, feeling that it is no place for the journalist to carry such a moniker. Pity.

If you accept a knighthood you accept the concept of honours. They are a non-monetary reward for people who make a contribution to our national life. The country meant them to have these titles and they should therefore use them.

Melvyn Bragg is hardly ever called Lord Bragg. Roy Hattersley blushes to use his life peerage. They should stop being such dainty violets (if we can use the word 'dainty' about cuddly Roy). Both are perfectly legitimate members of our Upper House. They should grasp hold of their handles with pride. Eco-campaigner Jonathon Porritt – that gulpy green with the unicorn bald patch – is queasy about his baronetcy but that is perhaps more understandable as it is a family title and he had no option but to inherit it. But there is no excuse for theatrical lefties like Sir David Hare and Sir Ian McKellen, knighted for their creative work. If they did not fancy the title they should have turned down the gong. So let us have 'Sir David' and 'Sir Ian' up in the neon lights outside the playhouse. Let's stop being so feebly common, to use the precise word. We all suspect that McKellen practised his 'Sir Ian' signature for years. Now he has the thing, let's use it.

Lord Lucan lookalike Viscount Thurso, a former Lib Dem member of the House of Lords, now sits in the Commons. He and his soupstrainer moustache ask to be known as 'John' Thurso rather than 'Viscount' or 'Lord'. Don't be such a limp lettuce, man. Lift your kilt and show us yer baubles! Thurso's lily-quivered approach calls to mind an A. A. Milne poem about Sir Brian

Botany, an aristocrat who is brought down a notch by his fellow men and becomes a whipped shadow of his former self. 'And he goes about the village as B. Botany, Esquire. "I am Sir Brian? Oh no! I am Sir Brian? Who's he? I haven't any title, I'm Botany; Plain Mr Botany (B.)"' Most of us would be proud of a family history such as Thurso's. We would feel honoured to maintain our ancestors' line. Yet in these days of class concern, these people slough off their titles like worms throwing a cast.

Mind you, there is every likelihood, if you do have a title, that class-ignorant journalists will only go and get the thing wrong, sometimes wilfully to show their disdain for rank. The failure of today's journalists to attend to the proprieties of titular protocol is a reflection of a silly belief that 'titles are only for toffs so don't really matter'. Thus, Life Peers are habitually written down as 'Lord David Perkins', whereas they should be 'Lord Perkins'. Only the children of higher nobility (e.g. dukes) take both the 'Lord' and the 'David'. Until we dismantle the House of Lords, we might as well get these titles right. The protocols are informative. To write 'Bart' or 'Bt' after the name of Sir Jonathon Porritt shows the reader the nature of his knighthood. Similarly, Lord Bragg is a Life Peer, a political appointment, a member of our legislature. Were he 'Lord Melvyn Bragg' he would be more aristocratic but less important. Being slovenly about the titles suggests that we are blithe about the power they indicate. Bad prejudice, bad journalism, bad citizenship.

Eliza's Lie

Written in 1913, *Pygmalion* needs updating. George Bernard Shaw's play has a flower girl taking diction lessons from pukka Professor Henry Higgins. Hurricanes hardly hever happen? How outdated can you get?

In my rewrite the roles will be reversed. A moth-eaten Prof Higgins will present himself at the dwelling of Eliza Doolittle, single mother of loose morals, bottle-blonde wearer of navel-baring designer t-shirts. She has been accommodated on one of those developments in the Thames Valley where the homes all look the same and the teenage boys have bull terriers. Higgins will be about to ring Ms Doolittle's bell (melody: a Britney Spears song) when a nose-studded member of the sisterhood staggers out, cursing, beer froth spraying as she opens a tin of Special Brew. This is Ms Doolittle's 'partner', en route to the benefits office.

Prof Higgins, having recovered himself, is soon explaining to Ms Doolittle that he has lost his job as a BBC pundit because his accent was 'too posh'. He has applied for jobs in the civil service, in the advertising world and at numerous quangos. All have told him that he is unemployable until he learns to 'speak proper'. Can the fragrant Ms Doolittle help him?

Eliza plonks herself down and, after extracting cash up front from her apologetic pupil, starts her tuition: 'nah' for 'no', 'to'ally unacceptable' for 'that seems a bit off', 'you must be facking jokin' for 'goodness me'. Before long Prof Higgins has an accent to match that of Radio 1 disc jockey Chris Moyles. He learns to drop haitches, drive the consonant 't' from his mouth and turn 'e' into something more like an 'a'. The word 'well' becomes 'wal'. Add some Geordie lilt, a twang of Australian interrogative uncertainty, a smidgen of Californian slang (adding 'like' in the manner of a chicken farmer spreading feed) and he is launched. The gracious old gent has been turned into a snarling, fulminating, formulaic product of the unhappy realm we know as bog-standard Britain. In a month Prof Higgins wins back his job.

It is not so completely impossible. Others have surrendered smart accents for something more of the moment, something more saleable. Some of our top politicians have affected rough argot to try to win favour. At Westminster select committees I have heard southern administrators come up with fake Tyneside voices, simply to show the Labour system that they have capitulated, have accepted the status quo. Now please don't hit me.

Good English should be our greatest asset. Here we are, a small island twenty-five miles off a polyglot continent, and our language has become Earth's lingua franca. How has twenty-first-century Britain responded to this windfall? It has steered for the rapids – look, rocks, over there, let's paddle over them and hole our canoe. Bog-standardisers have conspired to speak such a lazy, glottal-stopping, mock-northernised version of trashed-down English that the rest of the world struggles to understand it. When Scottish singer Susan Boyle was invited on to America's Oprah Winfrey show they had to subtitle her interview. There are recent Government ministers – Ian McCartney, Bob Ainsworth, John Prescott – who would need the same treatment before a mass American audience. Just as roses develop vigorous suckers which weaken their parent plant, so British English is allowing off-shoots to threaten its existence as an internationally understood language.

Our spoken English is in terrible decay. It is not just the poverty of vocabulary and idiom, for which we can blame rotten schools, poor newspapers, trash television and timid teachers. It is the slovenliness with which it is uttered, the mushrooming of diphthongs, the absence of tune and precision in the delivery as much as in the choice of phrase. Words are pushed around like over-boiled potatoes on the edge of a schoolboy's plate. Southern-voiced presenters say 'Lundun' for 'London' as though they are about to fall asleep. This never used to happen. It has spread only since New Labour started to proselytise for its northern heartlands. People who a decade ago would never have dreamed of pronouncing the final 'g' in present participles now do so. The Irish 'haitch' is breeding as fast as Florida mosquitoes. There is no appetite here for excellence, for surprise, innovation, for any distinctiveness other than a tenuous, semi-provincial class identity which buys the speaker a little Krays-style protection. Pride in spoken, cut-glass English has gone. Recognition as a leader of society now comes second to recognition as a member of the masses, as someone who has appeased the powerful northern English lobby – someone, that is, who says 'class' to rhyme with 'lass'. The idea of a national accent, of a linguistic version of Sunday best, has been cast aside in the chase downmarket. A few influential media controllers are trying to make us all speak like Salford typists. So paralysed are we by fear of 'snobbery' that we do not admit that every time a Radio 4 announcer or reporter hits a fake Lancastrian 'a', it makes us wince and, more often than not, turn off the ruddy BBC and listen to some classical music.

The British should be the greatest English speakers in the world – after the garrulous and still culturally jealous Irish, anyway – yet we plod through our sentences with tongues lolling. The overseas listener walks away baffled, disappointed, perplexed at our lack of pride. Many of our countrymen now speak a chameleon tongue which combines antipodean, North American and Celtic speech patterns. Accent soup, anyone? Yankeeisms proliferate, as do clichés and slang. Among office workers and computer geeks this might not matter much but it is also true of professional communicators: broadcast journalists, politicians, shop assistants, the clergy, even actors. One of the old caricatures of life was of the silver-tongued salesman, a chancer who could 'talk the birds from the trees' and sell you something you did not want to buy. When did you last meet such a man? Last time I tried to buy a laptop the 'sales executive' was utterly useless, talking in training-manual paragraphs and showing no spark of human interest in the customer.

Too many public speakers are unable to project ideas or voices. The Archbishop of Canterbury, a decent and holy man, is one of life's incorrigible mumblers. His counterpart at York, potentially an exciting figure, speaks with such a strong Ugandan accent that, if we're lucky, we stoppeth one word in three. The Leader of the Commons, Harriet Harman, drops repeated 'ers' and 'ums' into her Meccano-construct sentences, the oratory metallic. Continuity announcers on radio speak a language that might as well be cold coley on the slab. Supermarket Tannoys are in the grip of a manufacturing line of verbal tripe artists, their nasal accents compelling you to dump your trolley in the aisle and leg it for the car park, covering your ears. Phone-in guests stagger through non-sequitur by way of platitude, via mangled grammar and under-informed overstatement. They then have the ruddy nerve to wheedle, 'Know what I mean?' To which a despairing nation cries: 'No, we don't!'

Politicians are paralysed by fear of the unscripted gaffe. They have this terror that they might not sound enough like their constituents and so their accents become tortured, patronising pastiches, grating on the ear almost as badly as the voice of celebrity salad-dressing tycoon Loyd Grossman. Strategy consultants have told backbenchers that this sort of thing matters. They should try to match their vowels to the biggest number of swing voters in the constituency. 'Oooh, we've got to relate,' the MPs quiver, flubbing their lower lips. Pathetic. Voters don't want clones. They want political personalities. They want leaders. Look how gratefully they fell on Boris Johnson, a gorgeous exception to the dreary mainstream. It isn't Boris's policies they chose. It isn't his statesmanship or his piety (hardly!) or his non-existent acumen. It is his accent, snortingly posh. It is his defiance of the liquidised norm. What they like is his refusal to appease the equality mob.

The ghastly jargon of modern politics, managerial, relentlessly robotic, is the verbal embodiment of compulsory uniformity. This egalitarianism is the opposite of spontaneity. This elite language, as spoken by the office zombies of big-state government, is the sworn foe of fun. Thou shalt not be individual. Thou shalt speak like a Westminster clone and regurgitate pre-set phrases about 'stakeholder engagement' and 'empowerment' and 'knowledge architecture' and 'the third sector', all delivered in a lifeless, elite-averse tone. This emetic egalitarianism flows from a desire to impose party discipline – a desire to control – and ends up strangling the life out of the very system it hoped to dominate. The electorate has become so bored by the torpid terminology of professional politics that it has ceased to pay attention. Along comes a Boris and they vote for him because they know he will at least use different words and say something wry. We should demand bravery from our politicians and the courage to resist linguistic fads should be paramount.

Neglect of spoken English damages those at the bottom of society's ruck. Worried about human rights and accusations of racism, we do not make immigrants learn the basics of our language. They therefore continue with their own tongues. No wonder they huddle in their own little ghettoes and start feeling bullied. Teaching them English would be the best thing the state could do – far more valuable than being given tax credits or family allowances or community centres – yet the creed of multi-culturalism insists that all languages are to be celebrated. English must not be considered 'better'. Who can blame immigrants for retreating to their own linguistic quarters when there is so little language leadership? The members of our elite not only swear like Waterloo fusiliers but also refuse to speak the best version of our national language with confidence.

English was invented in this kingdom. It is our heritage, passed down by the likes of Shakespeare, Trollope and Wodehouse. By being born British we are effectively being thrown a double six to start us on life's board game. Our native tongue is the currency of international business deals and transport communications. Imagine taking delivery of a car with all the extras already attached. That is what it is to be born anglophone – or at least it was until we started to scorn eloquence in favour of class-conscious grunting.

First we allowed the Cromwellian tendency to do down the very phrase 'the Queen's English'. They changed its name to Received Pronunciation. Then they set about replacing it with approved regional accents – those with an echo of the ruling Labour Party. Celtic voices were encouraged on the BBC because they defied categorisation on the English posh scale. North-easternised English voices flourished, too – the fact that Blairism sprang from Co. Durham and its surrounds, of course, being no coincidence. Shopgirl Estuarine was smiled on, with enough of the Berkshire/Wiltshire office belt thrown in to distinguish it from the more dated Cockney of a Derek Jameson. The satirists of *Little Britain* fingered this new, bog-standard Britain accent brilliantly, its bolshy vowels accompanied by a flurry of hand movements, pouty lower lips and mental dimness. Yeah but no but yeah.

The BBC, driven by the daft creed of reflecting Britain back to its audience rather than the Reithian ideal of leading Britain to higher values, has been the main agent of accent change. Poshness and eloquence were dropped. Listen first to a *Test Match Special* of twenty years ago and then to its counterpart today. You will be amazed at how the thing has been ratcheted down, hauled off its linguistic pinnacle. We have gone from the Hampshire burr of the poetic, well-read John Arlott to the inane twang of an off-the-peg jockstrap called Arlo White. Instant switch off.

A David Attenborough would never be given a chance these days. He does not speak in a demotic enough manner. When veteran foreign correspondent Charles Wheeler died recently there was much breast-beating by officialdom (Wheeler was reliably liberal, you see) but no one stopped to admit that his crisp, dispassionate delivery would nowadays have seen him banished to the fringes of the World Service. They'd have given his stories to little Miss Busy Hands himself, Richard Bilton, he of the Alan Bennett accent and long denim trousers. Come the revolution, that bloody man will be first up against the firing-squad wall, I tell you.

Let's try another programme, *Countryfile* on BBC1. Ah, you think, a show about the rural idyll. Let's hear some contemplative shire voices. Let's bring down the pace from its urban scramble. Think again. The presenters are remorselessly jizzy, *Blue Peter* voices for a thirtysomething generation. The favourite word of all the presenters is 'absolutely', used so much that after half an hour it ceases to have meaning. They all do a great deal of gasping and whooping. Why such wonderment? Apart from the fact that it is fake – most of them will be on take eight or nine – should the awe not be left to the viewer?

Received Pronunciation is, or was, English without allegiances, exaggeration, frenzy or melodramatic stress. It is neither Dame Edith Evans nor Dot Cotton. It has seen a thing or two of the world and is unfazed by disaster. It is pure, educated, restrained, modulated, grown-up, demure, grammatically correct. It does not belong (as is sometimes alleged) to the gentry or public schools. David Starkey speaks RP but is not posh. Michael Buerk speaks RP but is no toff. Bruce Forsyth speaks RP but at the time of writing is still not Sir Brucie. The Queen's English is not the accent of Windsor or Balmoral or Sandringham or London's Mall. It is all of those places, a federal dialect giving all regions a chance. Nor is it intellectual. Some of its best speakers are commendably uncomplicated – even thick. This unifying, civilising, clearly understood accent is simply the voice of the citadel, a citadel we can all join. It is a citadel in which no claim is reported without being turned over and examined for value, like a porcelain cup in the palm of Arthur Negus. It is a citadel without favourites. A nation without citadel is vulnerable. A culture without citadel is, at its core, heartless.

RP is more democratic than the sort of accent fashion which currently holds sway at the BBC, where you are 'in' if you speak

Geordie, 'out' if you speak West Country, 'in' if you come from Wigan, 'out' if you hail from Henley-on-Thames. This idea of the BBC nowadays operating a 'diverse' policy on accents is untrue. They would not (thank God) give us a BBC1 newsreader who spoke like Ali G or shrieked in one of those sub-Los Angeles gang voices used by bum-fluffed Al Qaeda fanciers in the dodgier parts of south Yorkshire. Yet there is a large section of modern Britain that now speaks like that – probably as many as speak genuine Geordie. The rise of Scottish and Ulster accents on Radio 4 is out of proportion to their existence in the population. What we have here is a political ramp, a wilful plan to make the nation speak a more Labour-flavoured way. It is dressed up as an assault on the toffs – because they think no one likes toffs – but really it is a power grab by the bog-standard brigade, the anti-elitism dogmatists who want to weaken our nationhood.

Enemies of Britain have long misrepresented the Queen's English, caricaturing it as a Mr Cholmondeley-Warner affair. That is why the Nazis invented Lord Haw-Haw, the German propagandist with a far-back accent. Happily, Hitler's boot boys overdid it absurdly. If Haw-Haw had had a more reasonable tone – if he had been more like a real BBC announcer, in other words – he would have been a far more debilitating force.

The principle of a high-reaching, non-political accent for our society's administrators is a progressive one. Ministers who speak RP are less likely to play the class card or the regional-interests, pork-barrel card. And we come back to clarity. Clarity is now so little regarded that we have a BBC economics editor, Robert Peston, whose mad delivery, elephantine sentences and dubious editorialising may well have worsened the banking crisis. Clarity is now so little respected at the BBC that on programmes such as *Skins* and *Ashes to Ashes* – the Corporation admits this – a large proportion of the audience cannot understand what is being said. Background music is so overdone and the dialogue so aggressively trendy that viewers over the age of thirty haven't the foggiest what is going on. Jay Hunt, Controller of BBC1, told the *Independent*: 'It's a big issue and what the BBC should be doing is listening to the audience.' You're making TV shows and half your audience can't understand them? It's a big issue all right, lady. It's downright crazy.

In *Keeping Up Appearances*, Hyacinth Bucket speaks with a 'refayned' voice, never more so than when answering her electric telephone ('the lady of the hice speaking'). Today's middle classes are more likely to speak Mockney. Even royalty has succumbed. Prince Edward was not too possessed of modern Britain's comradely ways to refuse the title Earl of Wessex, yet he has acquired a form of English far removed from the precise diction of his childhood. He nowadays sounds more like an IT executive from Swindon than a member of the British Royal Family. The Queen has altered her accent, shifting it several notches down the posh scale. Her Majesty does not yet prattle like a Milton Keynes hairdresser but she is a good deal less icy, linguistically, than when she succeeded to the throne. It is just as well that access to the Crown Jewels is not controlled by a voice recognition device or she would struggle these days to get her hands on the Imperial State Crown for the State Opening of Parliament.

We can be comparatively relaxed about the Queen's accent, though. It is a relief not to have a monarch who sounds like Brian Sewell and she does still speak in a way that is recognisably regal, thanks to its calm pace and controlled emphases. Modulation is of the essence. Her Majesty has not caved in to that bane of spoken English, the Australian or American rising inflection – the habit of lifting the voice towards the end of a clause or sentence, as though seeking reassurance. They do it because it feels egalitarian, seeking the listener's continued consent. What jibbering frets we have become.

The principle behind Received Pronunciation is that there should be a form of spoken English intelligible to all, editorially unspotted, imparting no sense of bias. This simply cannot be said about dialects. Brixton gangsta-speak, for instance, has a strong flavour of anger. Brummie, one of my favourite accents, is considered by many people to be comical. Raw Dorset is a bit Archers. To understand the twirly, almost Cork cadences of a Western Isles accent you need to twiddle your ears like the tuning dial of an old Roberts radio. All of these are interesting sounds but they are not efficient for communication on national, licence-fee-paid airwaves. Being regional, they lack any flavour of citadel. There is a place for the provincial voice but it may not always be on network broadcasting.

The stress on words can be highly political. Frenzied excitement is demanded by station controllers. A senior executive at the BBC's sports department was heard to demand that coverage of cricket matches be made more peppery. 'Every ball must be an event,' he said, quite ignoring the fact that one of the beauties of cricket is its conservative longueurs when the sides are testing one another's patience and the spectator's eye can wander to the progress of a grazing butterfly. The spirit of cricket is aesthetic rather than commercial, but commerce, of course, is an insistent harlot and our cultural commissars surrender to it meekly. The BBC sports executive had his way and another little part of England's soul died. The demand for that change to cricket coverage, as so often when change is being justified, was that 'we need younger listeners' (even though younger listeners have a habit of becoming older listeners). Weather forecasts have fallen prey to the same manic demand to keep striking syllables in an 'exciting' and 'interesting' way. They no longer deliver their words calmly. They stretch with every sinew of their larynxes to become mini-Branaghs, so thespily do they perform. To counter any risk of snobbery they come over all chatty and giggly and use silly phrases, delivered in accents that would not be out of place in a Ricky Gervais comedy.

This anti-elitist hankering to be everyone's mate has been at the root of the decline in primetime British comedy. We have now reached a stage of atrophy, where Radio 4 comedians such as Marcus Brigstocke and Steve Punt and Andy Hamilton are as predictable as the tides. Mostly they glottal stop. They live in cities. They pretend to be poor, hold a sardonic view of manners, a negative attitude to the United States, have slumped shoulders, a secular contempt for religion and a probable hygiene problem. Today's comedians think that simply to radiate disorganisation and general adolescence is to be funny.

Here are the bog-standardisers. Here is the new Establishment. Is it not time someone mocked *them*?

Part II
Engaging the Brain

Quack Doctors

Degree day at a university in twenty-first century Britain. Graduates have assembled to accept their scrolls. Parents are in the audience, Dad with the digital camera he has not quite mastered, Mum with her tissues 'just in case' she cries. A flunkey stands on stage, ready to shout something in Latin. The ceremony begins and everyone claps as the young adults, some shy, others larky, walk to the front to accept their certificates.

Degree ceremonies are better attended than they were twenty-five years ago (I don't think I ever attended mine). On the face of it this celebration of youthful achievement makes a welcome change amid so much criticism of the young. Degree day is an occasion for family pride and mortarboard grins.

But then comes the moment when the master of ceremonies calls for silence and, with a great puff of the chest, announces the recipients of the university's honorary degrees. 'And our honorary doctorates this year,' he intones, 'go to . . .' And the crowd tenses, expecting the name of some international polymath with numerous and learned achievements to his credit. Who will it be? Internet inventor Sir Tim Berners-Lee? Pianist Alfred Brendel? Mathematician Sir Michael Atiyah? Dream on. 'Our honorary doctorates this year go to . . . Mr Dickie Bird, Mr Murray Walker, Miss Cilla Black and Monsieur Raymond Blanc.' With which the whole edifice of university intellectualism collapses like a bouncy castle the moment its electric blower has been switched off at a kiddies' birthday party.

Honorary doctorates could be the most prized academic possessions but in our egalitarianised education system their potency has been trashed. Think back to the row at Oxford about the honorary degree for Margaret Thatcher and you will recall what such awards once meant. Mrs Thatcher was in her pomp as PM yet she was deemed too anti-academic a figure to deserve an honorary doctorate in civil law. The dons would not stand for it. The college fellows were tigerishly jealous of the prize. This is a vital aspect of any honours system. The honours themselves must have honour. You may disagree with the Oxford dons' treatment of Mrs T. but you have to admire the seriousness with which they guarded their symbol of esteem.

Fast-forward two decades and we find Hon. Docs being handed out like Nectar points at a petrol station. The University of Warwick has given an honorary degree to Jennie Bond, who used to report on royal matters for BBC TV and later took part in a celebrity reality show (ah, 'celebrity reality', the perfect oxymoron). It is possible, I suppose, that Miss Bond is an amateur philosopher of distinction. It is possible that, beyond those perma-tanned, shiny shins and that equine smile, there lurks a brain to match that of the late Albert Einstein. What do you think? At Liverpool John Moores University they not only gave an honorary degree to *Blind Date* presenter and 1960s pop sensation Cilla Black, but also to Sue Johnston, an actress who appeared in the soap opera *Brookside*. Meanwhile, world-weary folk singer Bob Dylan was given a degree by St Andrews University. *The Sunday Times* reported that America's Dr Dylan had to stifle an almighty yawn during proceedings. The time zones they are a changin'.

Oxford Brookes University, more informatively known by its former name of Oxford Poly, decorated *Ab Fab* actress Joanna Lumley (this was before her Gurkha heroics) and Chef Blanc. Did he turn up at the degree ceremony in his kitchen aprons with a tall white hat and a plate of *bonnes bouches* for the fellows? The University of Surrey turned England's most frequently crocked rugby player into 'Dr' Jonny Wilkinson – for services to male modelling? – and the University of Hull honoured a footie ref, Pierluigi Collina, known chiefly for his bald head. Not to be outdone, Leeds University garlanded Jack Charlton, while the University of Wolverhampton summoned the pop group Slade to receive an honorary fellowship. Next time you hear Slade's 'Merry Christmas', do remember to bow. 'Dr' Noddy Holder!

Why should that baleful bully Sir Alex Ferguson be honoured by Umist and Manchester Metropolitan? Why should golf commentator Peter Alliss and actor Martin *Men Behaving Badly* Clunes and hyperbolic Murray Walker be given degrees by the University of Bournemouth? Ditto Sky News's Eamonn Holmes by Queen's Belfast, ditto Cat Stevens by the University of Gloucestershire. These people may all be well known and pretty rich, in some cases even affable. But should they be academic pin-ups? Or are universities pandering to populism? After the Ferguson business a spokesman from the University of Manchester's Honorary Degree Committee said: 'You don't honour someone just because they are famous. There are many things we do in the local community to demonstrate we are not an ivory tower.'

It seems unlikely any of these people would have been honoured if they had not been famous. As for the 'ivory tower' remark, what is wrong with being secluded and lofty? Is a certain remoteness from life's hurly-burly not the very function of a university? Manchester United, which Dr Sir Alex Ferguson runs, is the athletic equivalent of an ivory tower. That is why it wins so many trophies. It is elitist, ruthlessly selective, driven by competitiveness, the best in its business. Universities should aim for the same. Umist and Manchester Metropolitan – and all the other colleges which try to get themselves some cheap publicity by palming honorary degrees to celebs – might find that their own reputations shot up in value if they reserved them for the greatest scholars rather than the greatest box-office draws.

If our society is to retrieve intellectual dignity it must become stingier with varsity rosettes. A greater parsimony with honorary degrees would be a telling symbol of a more rigorous – perhaps we can even use the word 'testing' – approach. It would also spare us the ordeal of Dr Cilla Black with hand on hip, pouting up for the cameras at a ceremony which should have nothing to do with showbiz.

Third-degree Burn

ANY other country would be proud of Cambridge and Oxford Universities. They would be hailed as the epitome of national endeavour. Lists of graduates would be published in the national press – perhaps with admiring photographs of good-looking 21-year-olds in sub fusc opening champagne outside the exam halls.

It was not just the Varsity rugby match and the boat race which used to be covered by the national media. Debates at the two universities' unions attracted reporters from Fleet Street. The undergraduate politicians who addressed those debates sometimes became minor figures of note. Senior politicians do still speak in these debates but not in the same numbers. It was good for the youngsters at Cambridge and Oxford to be made aware that they were somewhere special. Privilege carried a burden of duty. Why should the undergraduates today feel any responsibility to lead a society which so crossly tells them they are not special?

Gordon Brown betrayed the low politics of the anti-Oxbridge bias when he took up one young woman's grievance in May 2000. Laura Spence was a seventeen-year-old who failed to gain admission to Magdalen College, Oxford. Miss Spence, daughter of a police constable and a teacher, was a pupil at a comprehensive school. She was photogenic and hailed from the north east of England, Labour's most tribal heartland. She had ten GCSE A grades. She even played the violin. Yet Oxford cast an eye over her and decided it could not offer her a place to study medicine.

Having failed to make it into Magdalen, Miss Spence was 'snapped up' – as the newspaper sub-editors were to put it – by Harvard. Mr Brown, then Chancellor of the Exchequer, was in a political mood. The Conservative Opposition had been having some success with populist sloganeering and Mr Brown fancied following suit. His Scots innards churned at the damage he could do to the bulwark of the English intelligentsia. With his one good eye he scoured the horizon like a Dalek with its central squirter, scenting the breeze for grievance, hungry for a chance to exact some revenge on the alma mater of his chief tormentor Blair. There has perhaps always been a little tartan corner of Mr Brown that regrets not having gone to Oxford or Cambridge. He had to settle for Edinburgh University, a fine place but not quite the very best. Envy: so often the egalitarian's fuel.

Miss Spence's Oxford application had until that point been no more than an upbeat local newspaper story, describing how the lucky lass was off to Harvard. Mr Brown, leaping in with both feet, chose a different angle. Claiming that she had been 'lost' to Britain, he declared: 'It is scandalous that someone from North Tyneside, Laura Spence, with the best qualifications and who wants to be a doctor, should be turned down by Oxford using an interview system more reminiscent of the old school network and the old school tie than genuine justice. It is about time for an end to the old Britain where what matters more are the privileges you are born with, rather than the potential you actually have.'

For neither the first nor last time in his political life, Mr Brown was speaking class-war baloney (his tactic: when in doubt, invent a stereotype of archaic privilege, just as he did with his repeated claims about 'gentlemen's club' practices in the House of Commons during the expenses scandal of 2009). The more the Laura Spence story unravelled, the smellier it became. We soon learned that Miss Spence's headmaster was a media-savvy American who sat on a quango. The Magdalen don who had supervised Miss Spence's application, Prof John Stein, was a Labour supporter who had a long record of trying to help state-school pupils, particularly in the north east of England. A furious Prof. Stein broke cover to announce that Miss Spence, far from being the best candidate, had come only eleventh out of twenty-three for the five vacancies the college possessed for medical undergraduates. Far from bombing in the interview part of the selection process, Miss Spence had actually done well. It had been her strongest performance in the various trials. And of the five successful candidates, two had come from comprehensive schools, three had been women, three had been from ethnic minorities (that such matters are even recorded is evidence of the political pressure colleges are under to comply with equality quotas). If there was a reluctance among state-school pupils from the north of England to apply for Oxford University it probably, said Prof Stein, had more to do with Labour's introduction of tuition fees.

Gordon Brown's outburst on the Laura Spence affair was factually wrong. And yet it worked politically. Labour's core vote, believing this guff, was invigorated. Mr Brown won friends in a north-east English heartland which until then had been largely Blairite. It improved his credentials with the Left of the party. Clever Miss Spence may not have been right for Oxford – few of us are – but she departed for Harvard and did perfectly well. She is now back in Britain. So much for her being 'lost' to this country. All Mr Brown did was nurture feelings of grievance and entitlement among people with legitimate claim to neither.

Exams: A Mugabe Economy

From play school to Oxbridge high table, education has been sapped, filleted, drained. The egalitarians have whacked it with mallets until it resembles a trainee chef's minute steak: a bloody mess. Recent moves against private schools by the Charities Commission are but the latest development. The Commission, in a blatantly political way, is telling prep schools they must offer more free places to children from poor families. This will make the fees higher for other families at such schools, making excellence more elusive. Another triumph for the social engineers.

Throughout education tests have been made less daunting. 'Access' has been 'widened'. Officialdom has been so addicted to equality that primary-school sports days have been made uncompetitive.

Concessions to a grungy social background are now legally part of the admissions process. This discriminates against excellence. University admissions authorities are under orders to favour applicants from state schools, the better to meet diversity targets. Private schooling may once have been a privilege but in early twenty-first-century Britain it is trumped by victim status. Why should anyone bother to strive for their best? Low standards now have their reward. They are a passport to success.

This rule encapsulates modern Britain's celebration of failure, its glorification of grot, its worship of the worst.

Durham University is one of several universities which now select students using a pro-minority 'mathematical formula' (no more scientific, one suspects, than the 'formulae' mentioned in transatlantic shampoo adverts). It gives weight to the average GCSE score of an applicant's school. The worse the school, the more indulgently Durham will regard its pupils. It is hard to think of a policy better designed to discourage teachers and drive parents away from the best schools. Why should any community patronise its leading academies when the Government bends the rules this way? If they want their young to get into Durham University they should send them to the worst school and play the victim card. Great.

What we are seeing here is a form of mad self-destruction, a bias against self-betterment. Militant egalitarianism is in the driving seat like Mr Toad at the wheel of his roadster. Honk honk! Loony coming down the highway. The process is party political, being bent to favour schools in parliamentary seats held, more often than not, by the Labour Party. We tolerate it only because we are terrified that if we defend good schools we will be called snobs.

The meddling starts in nursery schools, where they dress it up in woolly talk about Montessori methods and 'letting the children learn for themselves'. Ah, auto-didacticism, the time-honoured chant of common-room sloths. Let the little dears teach themselves so we don't have to bother. If Mr and Mrs Neanderthal had taken such a laid-back approach to tuition it is doubtful mankind would have survived. 'Let them learn to use the bow and arrow themselves, Grunt, dearest. It's so much better for them to learn to express themselves.' Exit mammoth stage left, unharmed.

Egalitarians, who regard assertive pedagoguery with horror, claim that it is their duty to step back and let toddlers show one another the lessons of life. Class hierarchy (bad thing) is abandoned and bigger groups mingle in a disordered minestrone of democratised gibbering (good thing). The chief benefit to the school? It need not employ so many teachers. Cheaper.

We progress to primary schools, where the teaching profession has been so thoroughly feminised that men are almost absent. Then to the secondary schools, their timetables dictated by a national curriculum and their cultures sterilised by the apparat's mistrust of eccentrics. There is now such a bewildering, dehumanising set of guidelines and best-practice methods governing adult conduct around children that schoolmasters have had the whimsy squeezed out of them. It is said that this is done in the name of 'standards' (bog standards) but it is as much about control. Systems hate individualism. They are suspicious of flair. The tradition of the batty teacher has pretty much gone.

My old prep-school headmaster, Colonel Mike Singleton of Colwall, Worcestershire, was a dapper autocrat (new buttonhole every day in his Prince of Wales checked, three-piece suit) who would patrol the school puffing his pipe. We lived in awe of 'Mr Michael'. Long before his hooded eyes hove into view we would be able to smell his tobacco and dive for cover. It was not just the Erinmore and the squeak of his brogues. Everything about him gave off a whiff of command. As an eight-year-old I was petrified of him. He was perfectly civilised. He never caned me. He only ever spoke to me sharply once, when I had written to Dunlop asking for some stickers (to write to commercial concerns was against school rules). He invited me to confess my crime, placed his pipe in his mouth and silently ripped up the company's reply in front of the rest of my class. Mortifying.

Mr Michael would drive us to away matches in an ancient Bedford minibus with no safety belts and with gaping holes in its floor. When he double-de-clutched to get the groaning Bedford up the Malvern hills, it was hard to know which produced more smoke inside the bus: Mr Michael's pipe or the leaking exhaust pipe which released fumes into the passenger compartment. We looked up to that man. We never questioned his authority. The moment he entered a room of children, silence fell. When his ancient labrador Perry died on a school walk we wept buckets, not just for Perry (a fat old pooch who would beg for scraps in the school kitchen) but also for dignified Mr Michael, silent in his grief. We realised that we loved the old man, much though he frightened us. Colonel Singleton was an unforgettable figure but I don't suppose he would have lasted long under the gaze of Ofsted and its doctrinal form-fillers. Passive smoking? Carbon monoxide poisoning? A dog presenting a hygiene risk in the catering zone? And all that before you even get on to the flamboyant pink buttonholes.

So set on egalitarianism are today's educationalists that public exams, the device for measuring scholastic achievement, have been devalued. It has become easier to acquire A grades. There are more of them than there were, proportionally, and the questions are easier. Because so many more children now acquire a large number of As, they inevitably try to grab more to keep ahead of the pack. Schooling thus becomes a vortex of satchels and assignments, more work, more revision, less time for games and youthful dalliance. We will soon reach the stage when school leavers, like the citizens of Weimar Germany or Robert Mugabe's Zimbabwe, need wheelbarrows to carry around all their certificates. Exam inflation is rampant and our children are nervous wrecks.

A 1981 ITV serial dramatising Evelyn Waugh's novel *Brideshead Revisited* depicted Oxford University as a paradise for rich young men. This cemented in the public's mind an archaic idea of Oxford student life. As far as the viewers of *Brideshead* were concerned, Oxford students inhabited a hedonistic idyll of punting, teddy bears, champagne and stately homes. At the time I was working in Oxford, sharing a house with my brother and two of his fellow undergraduates. Our grimy digs bore little comparison to anything shown in the Granada TV *Brideshead*, yet the stereotype of baroque indulgence created by that TV show stuck. Oxford undergraduates were toffs, end of story.

Politicians dabble in class envy. Two of the worst have been Sir John Major and that bulgy-eyed berk Ed Balls. Both employed anti-elitism for narrow political ends. Mr Major (as he was then) made endless play of his impoverished background. He went on about it so much you almost had to conclude he had nothing else to say. Strike up the violins! Peel the onion! Yet although Mr Major's father was a circus performer, the family was not much poorer than that of, say, James Callaghan or Edward Heath. Onetime Lambeth bus conductor Major was just more paranoid about his station in life. He was a class neurotic who declared that he wanted a 'classless society'. A country in which a circus performer's son could become Prime Minister was surely already far from classbound.

Prime Minister Major was absurdly quick to take offence, not just if he felt he had been patronised by colleagues but even if he had taken criticism from lowly journalists. He would scour the newspapers for ruderies and then leap up and down, howling like a toddler with a stubbed toe. This man had been Chancellor and Foreign Secretary yet he was unable to grasp the grandeur of his achievements and could see them only, as the egalitarian always will, as some form of career progression, some procedural entitlement. I was dropped from the parliamentary sketch of the *Daily Telegraph* after calling the new PM 'dreary'. Downing Street had been greatly vexed. 'Dreary' was apparently too haughty an adjective. My editor, Max Hastings, told me there would have been no such fuss if I had only called Mr Major 'unexciting'. Apparently that would not have made Mr Major's egalitarian sensibilities twitch to such a degree.

Sir John Major is a well-read man – he owns a complete edition of Trollope – as well as being numerate and logical. And yet he fell to this virus of low self-esteem. Inadequacy ate at his innards. Not having been to university, he was suspicious of graduates and soon exacted his revenge. His 1992 Further and Higher Education Act scrapped the difference between universities and polytechnics. Let them all be one. Let them be equal. Let them be ruined. Down came the rarity value and intellectual standing of universities, crashing to the ground like one of those Victorian factory chimneys detonated by the late Fred Dibnah. Also lost was the idea of the polytechnics as a specialised part of the education system. Leicester Poly became Simon de Montfort University (there was momentary panic when they realised that the original de Montfort had been a persecutor of Jews). Birmingham Poly became the University of Central England. Liverpool Poly became John Moores University, named after a gambling tycoon. The old Polys had been recognised as having a vocational emphasis. They trained people for professions such as engineering. Now that they were called universities, that vocational merit was dimmed. The impact on the old universities, meanwhile, was that they seemed less intellectual. With the Government deciding it no longer had to subsidise students, greater numbers of youngsters were paying more to attend colleges which were less scholastically focused. What a bog-up.

Ed Balls, son of a garlanded academic, aches to be blokeish. He himself is so full of brains that you can practically see the computer disks spinning behind his eyes. Mr Balls craves approval from the bottom of the pile. This would be an understandable and even noble aim in a politician were it not for the fact that he goes about it by wrecking the exams ladder with which the poor can clamber out of poverty. Mr Balls has presided over such a dilution of exam standards that some good schools now decline to use them. Once exams cease to be universal across the national system, their value to the poorest citizens is diminished.

Public exams have been hijacked by the equality crew and are designed for the duller pupils. Not that you will hear them called 'pupils'. Anyone over the age of twelve is now a 'student'. The old word implied subservience, someone unequal to the teacher, and was therefore dropped. Why do we put up with all this rubbish? Well, each small tug on the sail's ropes seems so small that it is pointless to complain.

I'm not sure I know anyone who believes there has been no grade inflation in exams in the past thirty years. And yet Ed Balls indignantly denies the possibility. Anyone who questions the notion of scholastic progress is accused of 'doing down Britain's hard-working students'. Every exam results season politicians 'salute' teachers and 'congratulate the students'. Even the Opposition parties utter this claptrap.

How can we consider GCSE biology to be a serious test of a teenager's knowledge when one of the questions asked candidates: 'Which is better for you – sausage in batter or grilled fish?' Or try this: 'When we sweat, water leaves the body through: a) kidneys, b) liver, c) lungs, d) skin.' In 2006 the Edexcel GCSE science paper asked the following poser: 'Our moon seems to disappear during an eclipse. Some people say this is because an old lady covers the moon with her cloak. She does this so that thieves cannot steal the shiny coins on the surface. Which of these would help scientists to prove or disprove this idea? a) Collect evidence from people who believe the lady sees the thieves; b) Shout to the lady that the thieves are coming; c) Send a probe to the moon to search for coins; d) look for fingerprints.' There was also this one: 'Many people observe the stars using a) telescope, b) microscope, c) X-Ray tube, d) synthesiser.'

Egalitarians have hauled down standards like sailors pulling in the mainsail. Sure, it has been done subtly, yank by yank on the ropes, but the only people who seriously try to deny that it has happened are Education Ministers such as the utter Balls.

For the past forty years the schooling of our children has been chopped up and fed in to the mixer marked 'equal'. It has produced an unthreatening, indistinct stew, most of the lumps long since liquidised. The whole point of exams used to be the gradation of intelligence – to work out who had done best by a certain point in life. The national good could be served and the best young chemists and engineers and doctors and so forth could be found for the future. At this point education stops being about theory and social equality. It starts to become a matter of life and death.

Universities are filling up with students who can barely do the academic basics. We used to talk of a teenager 'going up to university to read English'. These days the youngster will be 'attending college to take a course'. There is a subtle difference. To 'read' a subject was a loose term, allowing a range of material to be covered. 'Taking a course' is more prescriptive, more babyish. It is the terminology of mass production demarcated by a central authority. 'Taking a course' bestows a sense of entitlement. Once you have 'been on a course' you will 'get a job', just as the chick graduates to its battery cage in the egg barn. In such a world, the tutor's vocation is yielding to something more like managerialism. Colleges have become brands, commercial concerns. They used to be thought august seats of learning. Now they pump out press releases and employ chief executives who devise growth strategies and ten-year advertising plans. High academia has become commerce. The city of dreaming spires is now a cost centre.

Cowell's Circus Maximus

Television talent shows may not be high culture but they are, if you unwrap them a little, sharply political – and pointing in the right direction. Ignore Danni Minogue's appalling insincerity and Louis Walsh's simian handclapping. The philosophical undertow of these shows is pleasingly subversive. It plops a bomb right down the chimney of the equality freaks.

The cruelty of ITV's *X-Factor* and *Britain's Got Talent* is at times as sharp as the noise made by a schoolgirl's recorder. The rudeness of the verdicts is enough to make even a reactionary wince. Those auditions can be hard to watch when it is clear the applicant is to all intents and purposes mentally subnormal. On *X-Factor* judges Danni and Louis, led by sneery Simon Cowell, make little effort to conceal their derision, while on *Britain's Got Talent*, Piers Morgan delights in telling contestants they are 'repulsive' or worse. While some tuneless, wall-eyed wretch hops and skips on one foot, crooning a hideous cover version of 'My Way', the well-paid arbiters on these shows laugh and yowl and the audience joins in. They roll their eyes and pretend to stick fingers down their throats. They have no compunction about taking the Mick. Shades of the Circus Maximus.

Egalitarian neck-clutchers watch in horror. They have been reared – trained! – to enourage the feeblest talent and to adopt an 'everyone must have prizes' approach. For years they have applied formulaic, appropriate-behaviour techniques to the most glaringly obvious pupil inadequacy, drawing their faces into expressions of lopsided drippiness when children attempt any artistic expression. 'Miss, I've learned a song,' wheedles some plainly untalented stodge who has as much musical ability as a kicked cat. Modern classroom protocol demands that the authority figure show appreciation, offer encouragement and a 'very GOOD, Timothy', even when Timothy has just delivered a discordant, uninteresting, entirely meritless version of John Lennon's 'Imagine'. It probably made the teacher imagine nothing except child murder.

Talent shows have no time for this soft-hearted twaddle. *X-Factor* ruthlessly sizes up the abilities of contestants in the shortest time. They have perhaps fifteen seconds in front of the nation to seize their moment. It is a 'once in a lifetime chance'. Nail it, and they may, if lucky, progress to riches and fame. Blow it, and they are thrown back to life in bog-standard Britain's estates, to mingle with drug addicts and shoplifters and car thieves. Tough. On *Britain's Got Talent*, a bad act will not last more than perhaps five seconds before the red cross marks light up. You're a failure!

The eagerness of unknowns to put themselves up for audition and place their innocent necks on the executioner's chopping block shows that despite the worst efforts of the patronising elite, Britons are at ease with the idea of rejection on merit. They reason that it is better to have a chance to succeed than to be told you have got to lump it with everyone else for fear of upsetting the feelings of the least able. Popular telly's 'vote to save Wayne' syndrome demolishes the argument that academic selection in our schools and universities is unacceptable.

OK, Simon Cowell is on many levels an idiot. How a plainly intelligent human being can satisfy his intellect by poring over pop song lyrics all day long, God knows. But Mr Cowell's *X-Factor* is an assault on the limp-as-washed-lettuce creed that we must always encourage kiddies and never tell them they are dunces. It isn't just a visceral appeal to our sadistic tendencies. We don't watch it simply because we want to see the loser cry, tempting though that proposition may sometimes be when the reject is a previously cocky little squirt. We watch it for the satisfaction of the competition. In such surrounds, sheer ability can be remarkably refreshing. When the 'hairy angel' Susan Boyle wandered on stage in front of Mr Cowell, Amanda Holden and Piers Morgan, she was initially laughed at by the audience. Then she started to sing her song. Jaws fell open like the bows of a receiving mother ship. Britain really was shown to possess talent, all the better for being unexpected and untartified.

The same competitive air prevails at BBC TV's *The Weakest Link*. Nasty Annie Robinson, dressed like a Soho dominatrix, slags off the meatheads who fail to answer questions correctly and can barely disguise her glee when she sends them home 'with nothing'. The *X-Factor* has been around since 2004 and *The Weakest Link* began at the height of Blairism in 2000. I remember watching it for the first time one early autumn evening in my hotel during a Labour Party conference and being amazed by the roughness with which the losers were treated. After the dribbling, droning wetness of a Labour conference, *The Weakest Link* was gloriously forthright.

The Neronian-style appraisal of the talent shows – thumbs-up for survival, thumbs-down for execution – is largely absent from our schools and universities. The adult world of work, Heaven only knows, is short on clemency. If our schools took literally their duty to prepare tomorrow's generation for the unsentimental world of work, they would expose them to occasional humiliation and fiery tickings-off from the beak. That might sound heartless but it would sure as hell produce a generation of winners. It's time we catapulted Ed Balls out of the job and made Simon Cowell Secretary of State for Education.

Beyond Belief

Christianity has a redistributive message yet the professionals of egalitarian Britain are twitchy about organised religion. Alternative belief system? Destroy! They cannot bear the thought of a hierarchy of priests speaking from raised pulpits, bending down to the faithful to impart mercy. Hey, that's the secular state's role.

Jesus preached fairness – you could almost call him a Leftie – yet the one thing no Creator can be accused of is egalitarianism. Human beings are not born with equal abilities. We are not clockwork toys waddling off a production line. Quality control is pretty lax, thank goodness, or else most of us would have long since been rejected by some white-aproned angel wearing safety goggles and a hygiene-conscious hat. The fact that life can be so unequal is something believers have to confront and work out in their relationship with God. My own belief, for what it's worth, is that inequality is the natural way of things – part of nature's keyboard of high and low. We have different gifts in different measures. These strengthen the community and community, albeit a soapy little word redolent of sociology bores, is what most religions are about. Group worship is the physical binding of disparate talents. Church on Sunday is the merging of a congregation's unequal characters, forming something stronger than the sum of its parts. We could see it as a civic duty to attend, were duty a thriving concept.

Duty? Smelling salts, Marjorie, at the double! The egalitarian thinks duty a demeaning concept. Public service duty, military duty, political duty, parental duties – all these involve an idea that other citizens might require our help and that we might be in some way better equipped than them. That sets the egalitarian's nosetip a-tingle. It's why Thatcherism was so unTory. The Tory, being at one with class structures, has a firm sense of duty. Extreme Thatcherites, who hated the old class system, were driven by individualism. Like egalitarians, they thought duty outmoded.

So idle has our country become concerning the duty of churchgoing that religion is now something casually to mock, something for lads' nights out frivolity. In May 2009 a group of beery men from Bristol dressed up as nuns and processed through the streets of Crete. They were arrested for 'causing offence' – there were reports of football chants and mooned bottoms of pallid, spotty countenance. The following day, set free after a court acquittal and still all hairy-legged in their nun costumes, the Bristolians remained furious that they had been temporarily relieved of their freedom. The god of individual liberty (to do whatsoever I please, howsoever anti-social) had been offended. Spitting bitter words about their intention to seek legal redress, these representatives of modern Britain, the cream of Bristol, simply could not comprehend a society in which ridiculing religious garb might be considered sacrilegeous. In the dustier corners of Europe they still try to keep alive a sense of religious formality. Some Spanish cathedrals will not let adult men enter if they are wearing shorts. Visiting a church in Croatia last summer, my wife, who was wearing a floral strap dress, was tapped discreetly on the arm by a nun and asked to drape a cardigan over her shoulders. At least I think it was a nun. I suppose it could have been a Bristol japester on a fancy-dress weekend.

The equality industry is given the willies by religion – not just Christianity but other creeds, too. Egalitarians are determined to show the beardie Godbotherers who's boss. They therefore lend their bureaucratic muscle to organised secularism and encourage friends in medialand's liberal temples to project the cause. Never do you hear a broadcaster vehemently defend the consolations that religion can bring to the poor and the ill. Seldom do you find the *Guardian* admiring the commitment of thousands of priests – imams and rabbis, even though these underpaid servants minister to our needs at humanity's most vulnerable hours. State-employed counsellors on handsome salaries are regarded as saints, yet vicars on tiny stipends are condemned as spreaders of a dubious gospel.

The Equality and Human Rights Commission has given money to the British Humanist Association to 'explore issues increasing understanding of issues of religion or belief in the context of the equalities and human rights within the voluntary sector, media and general public'. You almost need to say a prayer before untangling such terminological spaghetti. What they meant was, we need to have a code about religion so let's get some atheists to write it for us. Terms such as 'exploring issues' are classic equality-ese. These people also love to talk of 'tools', or their 'work' or 'resources' and always list web addresses for 'anyone who needs further information'. For 'information', read 'indoctrination'.

The 'local campaigns officer' (another classic phrase) of the British Humanist Association, one Pepper Harow, sent out an email to 'practitioners in the equality field' about the work paid for by the Equalities Commission. Complete with internet links, Comrade Pepper's paper explained that the term 'religion or belief' was now to be used rather than 'religion' because it allowed non-religious beliefs to be included. Similarly, non-belief was to be embraced in all of officialdom's future considerations of religion. Between them, the Equalities Commission and the humanists cooked up a guide for local bureaucrats which included terms such as 'check your thinking' and 'check your language'. Most important of these was the stipulation that when discussing religion with the citizenry one must 'never assume that everyone has a religious belief' and that the term 'religion' alone should not be used. The 'legally correct, inclusive terminology' was now 'religion or belief'. Furthermore, all officials should 'include humanists when giving information about the "religion or belief" equality strand'.

Do savour that 'check your thinking'. Is there a more chilling phrase? Rinse it round your mouth as though testing a new-bottled Aligoté. Taste it on your British tongue. Does it not have an astringent tang? That is the authentic flavour of bog-standardisation. What 'check your thinking' means is 'make sure you think like us'. This frightening edict hints that organisations which do not give equal weight to atheists should not be permitted to do work for the state.

It is rare to catch the equality crew putting its wormlike tactics down on paper quite so baldly. Here is political correctitude emerging from the chrysalis – a U boat nosing out of the pens at Brest. Anyone skimming through the above document and its accompanying 'good practice guidelines on employment' might easily conclude that 'religion or belief' is now the only 'legally correct' way of referring to religion. Tosh. It is simply a loaded term produced by egalitarian atheists to undermine religion and to glorify lack of belief. This is militancy, wilfully political activity dressed up as egalitarianism – and all paid for by taxes.

Do non-regular churchgoers really want atheism to be held on the same cultural level as Christianity? I doubt it. Many people do not attend church simply because they are too lazy or busy or because they have a very faint faith. Maybe they have fallen out of the habit. Maybe they have taken a violent dislike (understandable) to modern hymns and the go-ahead liturgy used by some of the tinnier elements in the Church of England. But to demand that secularism be considered every time religion is addressed by official bodies is a bit like saying that every time a government body discusses sport it should give equal consideration to people who do not take part in any exercise. It is like saying that every time the Government subsidises art it should devote part of its deliberations to citizens who are uninterested in art.

Le Patron Worships Ici

A footnote to religion. At the front of a village church near us is a pew reserved for the local landowner and his family. It has been this way for generations. The family has been a generous benefactor of the parish church over the years. The walls bear plaques to the young men it lost in the Great War.

A generation ago that pew would have been full. Today it is often empty. The family still lives nearby but hardly ever comes to church. It would not have been like this in earlier times because the local 'squire' (a term seldom used now, for fear of upsetting those of us who are not squires) would have been the patron of the benefice. That is to say, he and his family would have been entrusted with selecting the vicar. This tied the landowner to the church, ensuring his attendance at services. This, in turn, meant that the village was more likely to come to church, that being a good time to make communal contact with the most powerful person in the village. Church was a time when the vicar could preach a pointed guide to clemency or generosity – speaking in code to the landowner in front of the village. It put the landowner gently in his place, reminding him of his duties.

Few benefices now have squires for patrons. Their powers have passed to the diocesan bishop, often a remote figure in the county town. It was felt that this was more democratic.

The old way of letting the grandee in the big house choose the clergyman was held to be an inegalitarian anachronism. After all, few of these squires had degrees in theology. What could they know about God? Anyway, they were unelected. They had no position in Synod. What could be equal about letting some ruddy-faced toff choose the priest? That was the thinking behind this change.

Now that the old patrons have surrendered their powers, they naturally have less interest in the church. They attend services less frequently and the hassocks in their old pews, decorated with their coats of arms, are being chewed by church mice. We might be tempted to argue that squires should attend church out of religious conviction but few rich men are naturally people of ecclesiastical devotion. Those of us who do still attend church do so for various reasons. I go because I like singing proper hymns and hearing the words of the Book of Common Prayer. I don't go simply because I have a hot-fire faith. What faith I do have, I derive from the rhythm of regular churchgoing.

The absence of the biggest farmer from village services makes other residents less interested in coming along to Sunday services. This makes the church less of a focal point and makes the vicar less respected. All this makes for a less congenial community. It is something the Church of England could improve by restoring the powers of patron to the local squire. Won't ever happen, I guess. But that is not to say that it shouldn't be tried.

Courting Disaster

Opening nights at the Royal Court Theatre are a great gathering of our bog-standardising elite. Just as the newcomer to Eastern Africa is encouraged to visit Treetops Hotel near Nyeri to see buffalo and bushbuck at the waterhole, so the newcomer to London should drop in on the state-subsidised Royal Court when it is unveiling a production. Here is the cadre of cool, the narrow opinion pool which sets taste in our dramatic arts.

Standing there sometimes in the basement bar – once a public lavatory and cottaging joint – I wonder what Sir David Attenborough would make of it in one of his wildlife films. Whispering in his hammy way, he would perhaps explain the scene. 'And here we see the leaders of the tribe in their natural habitat, coming together at sunset in a plumage of crumpled grey cotton and unwashed hair. They pout, yawn, cough. This is the mating ritual, a show of weariness designed to impress the opposite – sometimes the same – sex.' Sir David could note how they greet each other with high-five handshakes and say 'yo, dude' in fake Cockney. He could describe how they call one another 'mate' in an unenthused way. The aim of these creatures with their poached-egg eyes and pallid skin is deadpan indifference. They generally think they are tremendously go-ahead, imagining their default Centre Left views to be anti-Establishment. In fact they *are* the Establishment and have been for about forty years. Far from being rebels they are fantastically dull swallowers of a party line.

What a miserable, world-weary bunch they make with their clip-on exhaustion and their vegetarianised appetites. They paddle in the shallows, regurgitating dross because they daren't demand better. The age range at a Royal Court opening is limited. The majority are thirty-ish, not yet married, certainly not yet parents. Few of these first-nighters could be described as old or right-wing or indignant, even though vast swathes of the country are all three of these things. Nor do we find many here who are working-class. The audience does include a few City types who have removed their ties. The majority, though, if they work at all, are professional creatives, middlers from the media world, arts administration, the trendier charities, people employed to think the correct thoughts.

These first-nighters are often invited specifically because they can be counted on to make approving noises during the show. Take one recent such evening. The play was called *Grasses of a Thousand Colours* by an American, Wallace Shawn. His father once edited the *New Yorker*. Mr Shawn, now sixty-five, was brought up in a rarefied atmosphere, surrounded by his parents' witty friends. You would expect such a man to be civilised. You would expect him to have a well-developed aesthetic. But this is the decadent West. Refinement, my dears, is fantastically bourgeois. Mr Shawn, who was given an entire season at the Court, is a fount of low-grade scatology. I will need to go into a little detail, some of it graphic, to give you a flavour of this particular masterpiece. Those of a sensitive disposition should, as they say in sportscasts, look away now.

Mr Shawn, taking the central role in his own production, plays a scientist with a penchant for masturbation. His character walks on stage in a silk dressing gown and fancy pyjamas and starts to talk, at vast length, about some book he has written. The opening monologue is slow. This being the Royal Court on press night, no one shifts or grunts to indicate discomfort. The audience just sits there, stroking chins and offering the occasional murmur of appreciation. Ho ho. How droll. That sort of thing. It doesn't do to question the new, particularly if it is from Manhattan.

After about half an hour of dullness, Mr Shawn's character starts talking matter-of-factly about his penis. He talks, also, about vaginas and about how strippers at a club he knew once urged customers to pull out their 'dicks' and start pleasuring themselves. All of this is uttered, still, in a bland, nasal voice. The Royal Courters start to guffaw. Mr Shawn warms to his theme. He proceeds, over the next three hours, to describe adulterous affairs with two women as well as repeated copulating with a cat. 'Her paw extracted my member from inside my trousers and my astonished penis was completely enclosed in a warm coat of indescribable cosiness,' says Mr Shawn, with a lispy voice and too much spittle in his mouth. The more he dwells on sex, the more he sounds like a noisy eater with a bowl of minestrone. By now we are on to a seedy account of his feline coupling, even to the detail of how the sheets of his bed became stained.

Does the audience squirm? No. Several people laugh in a whoopy sort of way. Their ostentatious amusement may discourage others from expressing distaste, I don't know. A goatee-bearded man one along from me finds it so funny that tears course down his cheeks. The woman next to him keeps looking at his hilarity and, in turn, gives slightly uncertain smiles. Liberals sometimes talk of the tabloid press whipping up disapproval in society. Might it not be equally possible for approval, for tolerance of demeaning and vile behaviour, to be 'whipped up'?

These Royal Court goers are more than insiders. They are leaders of taste, commissars of our national culture. While we still have fine organisations such as the Royal Shakespeare Company at Stratford-upon-Avon we do have some protection against the Wallace Shawns of this world but it's a losing battle. Arts administrators have become so remote from the people who pay their wages that they feel no duty of leadership and do not pause to consider the damage they do with their celebration of the crass and coarse. I suppose I should have walked out loudly from the Shawn play, but theatre critics are witnesses and are therefore not supposed to do this, even if it means having to listen to further masturbatory fantasies and some gruesome stuff about the libidinous cat having its head severed.

At the end, as I fled for the exit, the audience was standing to applaud the bald, froglike Mr Shawn as though he was some maestro of high art. The following morning a couple of the more easily impressed reviewers gave this foul show four stars. They may genuinely have found it an enriching evening but I suspect their praise was fuelled by the desire not to look prudish. Fashion is sometimes little better than blackmail. Decadence is an infectious disease. It bullies the weak into accepting bad behaviour as the norm.

Broad Brush

Modern art started to go wrong when the curators stopped wearing corduroy jackets. They used to have thick-framed spectacles and Captain Haddock beards. They smoked pipes and generally behaved like something out of a Peter Sellers film. Nowadays they look more like doctors. Lean hips and cheekbones. Herr Flick glasses. Silken suits. The head of the Tate, Sir Nicolas Serota, could easily pass muster as one of the crueller types of anaesthetist. You can imagine him saying, 'This shouldn't hurt . . . too much.'

Today's art is incapable of expert execution. The idea is all. Concept is what counts. The ability to bring that concept to life might as well not exist. Damien Hirst employs artisans actually to do his metal bashing and shark pickling. Can it be possible that his ideas lean on other artists, too. There is little exceptional ability in Hirst save his flair for self-publicity.

Antony Gormley is one of our quirkier sculptors. His 'Angel of the North' is a vast, striking construction. His cast-iron figures on a beach near Liverpool have a similar sense of mute dignity. His idea for the empty plinth in Trafalgar Square, however, was a dreadful example of the diminishment of the idea of art. The vacuousness of the stunt would have been a wonderful joke had it not been quite so perfect an encapsulation of the bog-standardness of British art.

No one quite knew what to do with the plinth. Then Mr Gormley had (uh-oh) a 'great idea'. The plinth would be given to hundreds of 'artists' for an hour each. Anyone could apply. While on the plinth they could do what they liked. Some plinthers sang, some read books, some pretended to sleep. The simple business of expression, alone, was held to be artistic. I suppose there was a certain festivity about the stunt. But what did it tell us about art, save that these days anyone can do it?

This is the same principle under which the cold-livered Serota, a friend of Mr Gormley, has run the Tate for several years. Joyless, underfatted Sir Nick seems to hate figurative, disciplined art which has been crafted by skilled hands. It is as though he opposes the very flesh and breath of human concourse. He is in league constantly with the new and with shock on an unwieldy scale. If he can pull in the punters and show himself an impresario – trawling for custom – he is happy. Visitors to his Tate Modern are thus presented with objects so enormous and ugly that they naturally become a focus for discussion. But where is beauty in all this? Where is the excellence of brushwork or sculptor's casting? Where is the humanity? It is discarded because it will not seize headlines.

The Royal National Theatre recently staged *The Pitmen Painters*, a play which told of art's life-affirming powers. In Lee Hall's play (based on a book by William Feaver) a group of coal miners slowly learn how to paint. The process of acquiring that skill is as important as the end point of expertise, for along the way the men develop appreciation for beauty. They can step back and admire the skills they have acquired and they can think, 'Blimey, *I* did that.' They grow as people. *The Pitmen Painters*, like the musical *Billy Elliot* (also by Mr Hall) shows how art, if we work at it, can lift our lives.

Art at present seems to be simply a matter of short-term notoriety, of business contacts with a tiny knot of subsidised art curators. The pressure is to conform to the taste of perhaps three or four managers of state galleries. Unknown talents have almost no hope of becoming prominent unless they manage to work an 'in' with one of the Serotas of this world. Amateur artists become disengaged, feeling there is no point trying their hands at a daub if the art hailed by the egalitarian elite is so valueless. The skill of their fingers and their eyes counts for nothing.

That is the dubious achievement of today's British art supremos. By eroding the expertise of art, by dragging it into the mediocrity embodied on Mr Gormley's plinth, they have devoured its very being.

Channel Phwoarr

She might never have done it had she known it would keep Jon Snow in work, but Margaret Thatcher created Channel 4. In its early years the channel hauled terrestrial broadcasting upmarket. It was probably the most elevated mainstream TV channel in the world.

Channel 4 was led by Jeremy Isaacs, a tenacious Glaswegian who understood the educational possibilities of telly. Even better, he spoke in clear, complete sentences flavoured with just a hint of aggression. There was nothing slovenly about Isaacs or, at first, about Channel 4. The channel was told by Parliament to be 'distinctive' and from its first programme on 2 November 1982, the anagram and arithmetic riddle show *Countdown*, it set about the task. Mr Isaacs (later knighted) took 'distinctive' to mean lofty. He ran intellectual lectures presented by sideburned chinstrokers. He ran short films from abroad and an opera every month. The nightly news was more in-depth than could be found on other channels. Norman Tebbit, in a private meeting with Mr Isaacs a couple of years after the channel started, grumbled that the Tory leadership had actually had in mind something more like golf and yachting programmes (Denis Thatcher's tastes) but the Isaacs formula was permitted to flourish, even though the channel frequently irritated the ruling party. Channel 4 did not make much money but it was a *succés d'estime*. Watching it, one actually felt rather proud to be British.

Here was an attempt to use the airwaves responsibly and raise public gumption in a way the BBC had done before it fell to bog standardisers. Channel 4 was unashamedly elitist. Mr Isaacs had a notion that there were certain works of literature and music that should be offered to the public. Give the public a sober body of classics, not all western, not all ancient, but all excellent and enlightened. Penguin Books and Everyman's Library once did the same thing. This was snobbery of the best sort. It was leadership.

There was an audience, too. An early performance by Placido Domingo was seen by more than two and a half million people. Even audiences of 100,000 for less commercial operas were some fifty times bigger than the Royal Opera House could squeeze under its roof – and more than ten times the size of the old Wembley Stadium. Channel 4 represented an ideal of arts subsidy, feeding audiences who lived too far from the capital to attend live performances. Even Channel 4's philosophy programmes at 11 p.m., featuring polo-necked thinkers such as George Steiner and Al Alvarez, scored six-figure audiences. Amazing, really. Other broadcasters saw what was going on and thought, 'Hmmmn, perhaps we should try that' or 'We'd better not plunge too downmarket because compared to Channel 4 we'll look disreputable.'

Sadly, this noble vehicle was steered off the road. Mr Lowest Common Denominator himself, Michael Grade, he of the sod-you cigar and the showbiz braces, was chosen to succeed Mr Isaacs. He had no liking for the channel's top-end arts coverage and within days of arriving scrapped several shows. He also ordered that Channel 4's schedule should have the same major 'junctions' (i.e. time chunks) as ITV. This boxed in the programme makers, trimming their freedom as though with a savage hedge cutter. In came American sitcoms. Ratings rose a little. Distinctiveness plummeted.

One of Mr Grade's acts of warped populism, a year before he left Channel 4, was to introduce Chris Evans's *TFI Friday*, a show of celebrity interviews and reheated parlour games. One of them was a rip-off of *Who Wants to Be a Millionaire?*. The only things 'distinctive' about *TFI Friday* (the name allegedly stood for 'Thank Four It's Friday' but the second word was obviously meant to be something else) were its crudity and childishness. Drunkenness, bad language, vandalism, cruel humour at the expense of children and blameless civilians – in general, the worship of crassness – were the hallmarks of this rotten little show. It made money, of course, because it was appealing to viewers' worst instincts. Evans later sold his production company for some £290 million. It is no great surprise to learn that Chris Evans is a firm friend of Jonathan Ross, another graduate of Michael Grade's Channel 4.

Channel 4 News survives, as does *Countdown*, but much of the channel is now property pap or lewd rubbish such as *Big Brother*, an interesting idea overdone. Michael Grade has long gone (since then he has also had miserably lowbrow spells at the BBC and ITV) but the effects of his grotty spell in command continue to be felt. Ruddy man.

In June 2000 Mark Thompson, then director of television at the BBC, gave a speech in Banff, Canada, at which he suggested that 'elite culture' no longer had a place on mainstream TV and that with digital channels it could be parked in 'niches'. Mr Thompson spoke of arts and current affairs as 'difficult' genres and seemed unimpressed by the idea that a television channel might juggle popular programming with some more elevated offerings. This was, in effect, a relinquishing of any sense of patriarchal responsibility in broadcasting – something on which the whole BBC public service ethos is based. If we shunt arts programmes to a different digital channel we are giving up on the idea of explaining British and European civilisation to our children. God knows, in today's egalitarianised schools they have been taught precious little. If they never understand the history of Christian culture, how can they be expected to understand the roots of our tolerance – the very tolerance which is so often prayed in aid by egalitarians?

If the public sector broadcasters go all bog standard and give up on the arts, what is the justification for the BBC licence fee? Mr Thompson and Co., over-impressed as they are by market research, approach the argument from the other direction. They say that unless the BBC hits high ratings there can be no justification for its licence fee.

We should stop seeing the BBC licence fee as a broadcasting tax. It should become a cultural tax, a charge which says, 'this is the price of living in a civilised country', this is a tax for moulding moderate and enlightened attitudes in our fellow subjects. Ratings are nothing compared to the value of having palatable, honest, noble programmes. Bog standards are death to the BBC and it is miserably depressing that the same, stuttering, jargon-spouting Mark Thompson, with his wet terror of instinctive leadership, went on to become head of Channel 4 and then director-general of the BBC (the director-general who tolerated Jonathan Ross's bad behaviour). The man is palpably unfit for his high office in our culture. We can only hope that one of the first acts of the next Government will be to order his dismissal and, while they're about it, find a BBC chairman who will unashamedly declare, 'Our culture is worth celebrating and worth fighting for.' Why not Charles Moore? God, that would shake them up. Chairman Charlie!

Bum Rap

Rap music glamorises guns, takes a low view of women and is not really music at all. It is, however, much encouraged by comfortably off, liberal whiteys. Why?

We could be generous and say that rap has reintroduced the notion of rhyme to poetry. Sadly, the rhymes are seldom audible, so closely do rap singers hold the microphones to their mouths, causing 'popping' and sound distortion. The rhythms of rap are not particularly interesting. The predominant metre has one line of about five beats, followed by another of seven, this pattern being repeated ad infinitum. There is another with an ankle-tripping gait. And that is about it. Stedman's 'How They Brought the Good News from Ghent to Aix', with its thrilling evocation of a horse's galloping hooves, this ain't.

The reason rap is pushed down our ears is that it is seen as the music of the black street youth. Radio stations and advertising executives are desperate to appeal to that minority, not because they have spending power but because they are a minority and can therefore tick a diversity box. Given the frequent anti-homosexual content of rap, equality practitioners regard it with trepidation. They want to approve of it yet they dare not. So far, rap has suffered little political criticism. Gay rights has, to its dismay, been unable to trump black rights.

How come? Well, gay people are generally seen as being more middle-class and privileged than black teenagers. Outproled!

Ben Summerskill, head of the gay lobby group Stonewall, horrified MPs when he gave evidence to a parliamentary committee considering 'hate' laws. Mr Summerskill was asked to give examples of incitement to hatred of gay people. He did so with knobs on, if we can put it like that. Mr Summerskill: 'There is an artist called Beenie Man who has produced a record called "Hang 'em high", which includes the lyrics "Hang chi chi gal wid a long piece of rope".' Smiles of gaseous uncertainty from the MPs and clerks. Mr Summerskill: 'The key lyric in that means, "Hang lesbians with a long piece of rope". The same guy has created a single called, "Batty Man Fi Dead", which essentially means that gay men should die.'

He continued: 'Another single is a song called "Roll Deep", of which the key chorus is "roll deep motherfucka, kill pussy-sucker", which is a reference to lesbians. It continues "tek a Bazooka and kill batty-fucker", which means, "take a rocket launcher and shoot gay men dead". An artist called Buju Banton has produced a single called "Boom, Bye Bye" which essentially means "goodbye" and again involves encouragement to use an automatic gun to kill gay people.'

By now the stenographer from *Hansard* was the only one person in the room remaining completely expressionless, but that was only because she was having to concentrate hard on her machine, making sure she pressed the right buttons to convey lines such as 'faggot fi get copper to di heart' ('copper' being rap-speak for a bullet), 'batty bwoy stand up anna talk and man a park', which is a disobliging reference to a gay chap talking to someone in a park, and 'a wet yuh up wid di Maggy' which I believe means 'I will kill you with a Magnum' (a Magnum gun, that is, not one of those rather oversized Magnum ice creams so popular in obese Britain). As Mr Summerskill explained, this sort of music is not just found in obscure bars and clubs. It is available on the internet, even on Amazon.co.uk.

Some people, particularly gay men, will wonder how rap record producers and Caribbean culture can continue to pump out this sort of agitprop without attracting the attention of the police. After all, author Lynette Burrows was leaned on by the constabulary after making some pretty mild remarks on BBC Radio Five Live. All she had done was question the right of male gay couples to adopt baby girls. The rozzers swooped on Mrs Burrows on the grounds that a 'homophobic incident' had been reported. Scotland Yard confirmed that homophobic incidents were 'a priority crime'. So how come rap musicians get away with it? This may have something to do with the fact that their words are hard to understand. There is also the valid argument that to sing a song about killing a person does not necessarily endorse that activity. Think of Eric Clapton's 'I Shot the Sheriff'. And yet it is hard to escape the conclusion that the police leave rap music alone because it has more minority value than the gay people it so charmlessly attacks. Lynette Burrows was collared because she was an easy target and because she was one of the majority. The rappers are more frightening and they have the political Scotchguard of victimhood.

Is there, in effect, an unofficial pack of equality Top Trumps cards? In egalitarian Britain, who has the best minority credentials?

They could go something like this:

LESBIANS AND GAYS

Media connections	9
Victim status	4

Rarity value   3
Fear factor   6
Political/financial clout   8

MUSLIMS
Media connections   4
Victim status   6
Rarity value   4
Fear factor   9
Political/financial clout   4

JEWS
Media connections   9
Victim status   8
Rarity value   6
Fear factor   5
Political/financial clout   10

DISABLED
Media connections   2
Victim status   9
Rarity value   8
Fear factor   1
Political/financial clout   2

GURKHAS
Media connections   7
Victim status   5
Rarity value   6
Fear factor   9
Political/financial clout   4

TRANSSEXUALS

Media connections	1
Victim status	3
Rarity value	10
Fear factor	2
Political/financial clout	1

Part III
Out of the Office

Do They Mean Us?

Foreigners retain a touchingly generous image of the British. They often imagine us as people of gracious airs, opening doors for the infirm, standing when strangers enter the room. We say 'please' and 'thangyew' and 'don't mention it – I insist'. Overseas caricaturists draw Britons as fastidious dressers, the men attired in Savile Row suits with polished brogues and a furled brolly, the women modest, twin-setted, pearled. We drink tea from fine china cups and lay the table for breakfast, complete with marmalade spoon and cruet. We address each other by our surnames, using respectful 'Mr' this and 'Mrs' or 'Miss' that. We read Beatrix Potter to our obedient, soap-scented children.

No we don't! When did you last see a twin-set? When did you last see a British woman blush? As for 'Cruet', he's that new French striker signed by United. We have become a nation of hard-ball hedonists, groin scratchers, beer-bellied burpers in armpit vests. We are gripped by a nasty sense of entitlement and a determination at weekends to 'have a good laff' (i.e., bash our brains with alcohol and then skirmish with strangers). It's our spare time and we'll wreck it if we so desire.

In play – games, fashion, gossip, romance – we have developed a nasty selfishness. The sense of common purpose, of social respect and comradely sodality, has been abandoned for something earthy and low-grade. Why should we care what our neighbours think? They're no better than we are. Selfishness for all. We've all got our rights. One of those rights is to use our spare time for self-destruction rather than self-improvement.

There is little place in such a society for civic leadership. The egalitarian is horrified by mayors who wear chains of office (archaic symbols of aggrandisement, see?) and particularly hates the brotherhood of Masonic lodges. They may do vast amounts of good work but the Masons are spurned by the modern Establishment because they contravene the equality code in numerous ways. They are all-male (no!). They subscribe to the idea of a Supreme Being (no! no!). They are mainly middle-aged business types who probably vote Conservative and call waitresses 'love' (nooooooo!). The great thing about Masons, so far as I can see, is that they have no time for fashionable tosh and they ignore these slights while continuing to dispense their philanthropy. It strikes me as almost wicked that they should have been so condemned by the received-wisdom gang who themselves seldom contribute to communal well-being. I should add, to quell the inevitable conspiracy theorists, that I am not, nor ever have been, a trouser-roller. I just happen to think that the Masons are generally an admirable organisation, quite untypical of modern Britain.

Volunteerism springs from a sense of self-value. The generous people who run Brownie packs and church groups and boys' sports clubs derive satisfaction from feeling that they have lent their talents to the community. This self-esteem is resented by the careerists of the equal opportunities industry who are suspicious of citizens who consider themselves a cut above. It is sometimes as though officialdom is determined to make life as difficult as possible for worthy outfits which have bumbled along as amateurs for years. The professionalisation of charities – which have been

given their own, Berlin Airlift-style name of 'The Third Sector' –
has dimmed what was, for many, an enriching experience of
amateur work. The regular churchgoer is told he or she may not
mention Christian beliefs when doing unpaid work with British-
Asian children because it might offend their culture. The young
parent who offers to help at an after-school club for toddlers is
subjected to a demeaning Criminal Records Bureau check because
equality means that discretion may not be applied. The
octogenarian mother of BBC Radio Five Live presenter, Nicky
Campbell, is prevented from taking snapshots of her grandchildren
at an Edinburgh swimming pool owing to some apparent suspicion
that anyone photographing children is a raving pederast. The
official on the spot would not use common sense and think 'there's
a granny taking a happy family shot.' To do that, you see, would
be 'discrimination'.

Our better people – and they *are* better, even if we're not meant
to say so – have lost the impulse to try to lead communities because
they reckon the System resents them for being normal. The male
volunteer who offers to take a small group of boys on a weekend's
camping trip is surely scouting for trouble. No-win, no-fee laywers
will be down on him like jackals if any child suffers an injury. And
that is before the nasty, smirking rumours start about what
happened in the tents at night. In the world of equals, everyone's
a pederast because no one can be excluded from suspicion.

Civic leadership used to be driven by a worthy desire to help
other, less fortunate citizens. This has been pressed out of us by
the social pulveriser of egalitarianism.

Par for the Coarse

It is sometimes claimed we are 'all middle-class now'. Not true. Many of us are bog-standard class, dingy in our habits, lazy about propriety, careless of disapproval. We feel little compunction about eating and drinking in the street and at weekends some think nothing of lying a-bed until noon. Many is the wastrel who remains in his skimpies until lunch, hair askew, chin unshaved, emerging from his pit only to slope down the pub for a few bevvies in front of the satellite TV football. It's life, Jim, but not as you'd want your child to lead it.

The twenty-first-century weekend aesthetic is, 'why should we bother to tidy ourselves on days off?' There is no ranking to fear. Social climbing, once an improving rod for our backs, has vanished from large parts of urban society. When it comes to mufti and leisure time, the cry of modern Britain is 'one for grunge and grunge for all'. Foreign tourists arrive here expecting something out of an episode of *Miss Marple*, only to discover scenes closer to Stanley Kubrick's *A Clockwork Orange*.

We cannot look to the young members of the Royal Family for much of an example. Having been told by Leftists that they should behave like a 'bicycling monarchy' and that they should be more like their subjects, Princes William and Harry go boozing at London nightclubs and seem happy to be photographed leaving in the early hours, eyes half closed, clothes crumpled. Their friends say, 'Give the guys a break – these are young military officers having some R and R.' We are told this behaviour shows what well-adjusted, ordinary Joes they are. But this climbing down into the gutter is a dangerous tactic, for the other residents of the gutter may very well soon say, 'If you are joining us down here, why should we regard you with any awe?' The magic of monarchy may not last if this faux egalitarianism is pursued too long by Clarence House. Royalty and equality cannot co-exist. Let the princes drink all they wish but let them do it away from the public gaze.

While the princes set a crass example to other young men of their age, women no longer leave the hell-raising simply to the boys. They join in, trying to match their men mojito for mojito. They have lost the centuries-old idea of being demure in public. The sort of slender-lipped, self-questioning, hesitant lover played by Celia Johnson in David Lean's 1945 film *Brief Encounter*, is now found only in recently arrived immigrant families. The native British girls have become fat-faced 'ladettes', goose pimples rising on the skin of their exposed thighs as they clack-clack-clack along the pavement en route to the weekend disco, destination bonk. If they are really lucky, perhaps they will bed a prince. Older generations would call these women 'slappers' – and they would be right. Before the night is out, some of them will be bending over an open sewer, puking, weeping, wailing ''e don't love me!' before passing out under some sulphurous street lamp. Paaaaargh for the coarse. This is the twenty-first-century British way, a grottiness not seen on this crowded island since the early 1800s before Sir Robert Peel formed his police force to tame the grottier purlieux of London.

Women drink because they are trying to show how free they are. Here, sisters, is an unwelcome dividend of female emancipation. Liberation has led to loucheness, a way of life which brings its own imprisonment. Emmeline Pankhurst would be horrified but this is where the remorseless quest for rights has taken the fairer sex. It has overshot liberty and landed in a sweaty jungle where women are equal to men in squalor and excess. They are expected to get as plastered as the blokes and any girl who sticks to a nice pineapple juice will be unfairly mocked as 'frigid'. In a century we have gone from an over-genteel society which covered table legs to the other extreme in which girls publicise their sexual availability by wearing t-shirts baring their flab-mottled bellies. Four hundred years ago William Shakespeare depicted this type with his 'country copulatives' in *As You Like It*. There was one difference. In Shakespeare's day the gap-toothed country girl offering easy pleasure would later exact her price – the ball and chain of marriage. Yet thanks to the messianic toil of the equality crowd, marriage has gone down the khazi, discarded by scowling intellectuals as a form of religio-sexual bondage, institutional sexism minted at the altar of a male-run religion. And so women have been denied the financial and romantic security which came with marital vows. Women's lib gave men an excuse not to make a commitment and many of them promptly took it.

Hogarth's Inheritors

Two years ago the Tate Gallery in London (the real Tate – not that warehouse of valueless baloney near Tower Bridge) mounted an exhibition of the work of William Hogarth (1697–1764), whose oils and etchings of London life depicted the cruelty mankind does to itself in troughs of self-indulgence. We like to look at Hogarth's drawings with their harlotry and drunkenness, the warts and black spots of sexual disease, the pickpockets and fisticuffs, the filthy drains, and congratulate ourselves on our superiority. Or at least we used to be able to do that. Look at Hogarth's work in all honesty and you will see we are repeating the depravity of those days. In his 1751 picture 'Gin Lane', a bare-breasted drunk has so lost control of her senses that she does not notice her child is tumbling over a high drop. She could easily be one of the slatterns depicted in Paul Abbott's powerfully forthright TV drama *Shameless*. Some conservatives look at *Shameless* and worry that it is spreading the amorality of its feckless characters, the Gallaghers. I disagree. The great value of *Shameless* is that it offers a looking glass to Britain just as Hogarth did. We may think we do not have a gin epidemic, as Britain did at the start of the eighteenth century, but that is only because gin has fallen out of fashion. With its echoes of Empire, it is considered too posh a tipple for today's boozers. What we have instead is an alcopop epidemic, a vodka epidemic, a white cider epidemic, worst of all a crack and heroin epidemic. The art of William Hogarth shows a land where women, in particular, binge themselves and their unborn babies towards hell, damnation and an early grave – just like today.

It was not like this sixty, fifty, forty, even thirty years ago. So what happened? Well, alcohol became more affordable. Politicians eased licensing laws. Drinks companies came up with sweeter potions which they sold in colourful bottles. Beer and wine were strengthened. Most of all, equality campaigners demanded that women be treated the same as men – indeed, that they *were* the same as men – and drinks advertising hurried to show women knocking back the wets as fast as their boyfriends. The old habit of the man ordering himself a pint and 'a half-pint for the missus' became a thing of the past. Flo Capp, wife of the old *Daily Mirror* cartoon character Andy Capp, would stay at home when her dissolute husband went drinking. These days Flo would be alongside Andy, draining her glass like a suction pump, yelling 'get 'em in, girls!' And the drinks are now spirits, more often than not, rather than pale ale.

When I started as a reporter in the mid-1980s, women were not expected to approach the bar at Fleet Street's El Vino. In part this was because the men felt, in an old-fashioned way, that they should pay for the drinks (to be more precise, they felt they should stick them on expenses and get Conrad Black or Rupert Murdoch to pay later). In part there was also a feeling that it was improper for women to sink to the level of the men and fill their gullets with alcohol. Such alco-sexism has now disappeared. Younger women have lost all shame about drunkennness. To return to the pioneer feminist Mrs Pankhurst, she would surely have been horrified. Although she was driven by a quest for women's suffrage, she accepted that there were higher loyalties. When the First World War broke out, Mrs Pankhurst temporarily cast aside her political campaigning and redirected her howitzers (as she almost certainly did not call them) at the Kaiser. In the matter of women's drinking, Mrs Pankhurst and the suffragettes felt alcohol was the foe of emancipation. It took money out of family budgets. It turned men violent. For it now to be considered a woman's privilege to get blotto on Bacardi Breezers is a warping of the suffragettes' efforts. It is dismaying that Labour, of all parties, should have hastened the process by making it easier for working men and women to visit pubs. What happened to the Labour Movement's Methodist links? What happened to the quite proper idea that Labour's parliamentarians should show leadership and save the poor from the demon drink? I'll tell you what happened. It was a misplaced idea of equality, a sense that the poor – and women – should be able to drink as much as the rich. There may have been something noble at its root, but this was a terrible mistake.

That refusal to lead has brought us the New Gin Lane. Visit a British city centre on a Friday or Saturday night – witness a hen party advancing down the shopping precinct of Bournemouth, the once-genteel Dorset town which has contrived to become the hen party hot-spot of the country – and you will find that alcohol is the handmaid of female sexual swagger. Groups of twentysomething girls teeter along in impossible heels and hurl lurid challenges to solitary men. Attending political conferences in Bournemouth as just such a solitary man, I have found myself mooned by gaggles of boozed-up hen-nighters. A ripe eyeful, I tell you. Our Patterdale terrier bitch behaves in much the same way when she is on heat, moaning and whining and begging to be let out of her cage to get at the local farm dogs. But she is a dumb animal and has no concept of morality. Call it sexual confidence or liberation if you prefer, but who or what brought about this transformation from Celia Johnson's *Brief Encounter* character, Laura Jesson, to such Amazonian lewdness?

Aussie Miss Rules

One woman who must bear some of the blame is Germaine Greer, the freckled sheila who came to Britain in the early 1960s in search of fame, fortune and most of all headlines. To her, feminism was about a declaration of sexual power and she began arguing that case in newspapers, books and on the airwaves. Women had to assert their sexual hunger in order to claim their rightful place alongside the hump-and-dump men. To prove her point, Miss Greer set about the traditionalists of 1960s Cambridge rather as the brown-shorted, cork-hatted settlers of Tasmania once loaded their hunting rifles and went after the short-eared possum and the nose-boned abo. Bang bang. That was Germaine's tactic. Wham bam bang.

This dinkum thinker posed in fields in her underwear, sometimes less, to plug her books. She seized up and discarded men like a tramp investigating old sandwich wrappers in a municipal rubbish bin. It was her prerogative as a woman so to do. Women had the right to misbehave. Miss Greer, by flaunting her bosooms and spitting out men as disposable sex objects, may have created a lucrative career for herself. She may have enabled women to cast aside horridly uncomfortable 1960s brassieres, instruments of near medieval torture.

There was, though, a price to pay. One consequence of her convention-shattering ways was a destruction of modesty and decency. Hedonistic? Exciting? Novel? Daring? Germaine Greer's glory days were all of those. But the loss of dignity they entailed meant that the standing of women deteriorated. With that, the conduct of men worsened. They no longer felt they owed their female acquaintances any sort of behavioural discount. It was not just minor things such as no longer bothering to open doors for women or standing when they entered a room (as I was certainly taught to do). It was more disagreeable than that. Statistics suggest that violent behaviour against women – and even by women against men – has risen. If women were to be treated equally, as loose-knickered Miss Greer demanded, surely it became no worse to hit a woman than a geezer. So certain cavemen seemed to think.

Germaine Greer and her bank account may have been the winners but the losers were civility and gentlemanly conduct. The very notion of being a gent was redundant if men and women were the same. When the RMS *Titanic* sank in 1912 a large proportion of the female passengers survived but 80 per cent of the men on board went down with the ship, doomed by chivalry. They had observed the code of 'women and children first' to the lifeboats. Would that happen today? After the onslaughts of sexual equality, it seems unlikely. Anyone using such a term on a modern-day *Titanic* would probably find himself rapped on the shoulder by the ship's diversity champion and told he had uttered a sexist comment which would be investigated by the relevant authorities, just as soon as the lifeboats reached land.

The thing about Germaine Greer is that she was selfish. If she had been on the *Titanic* it might not have been a case of 'women and children first' but 'outta the way, cobber – Germaine's comin' through'. She was (and remains) a gloriously rude old boiler who produces a hot steam of egotism. In her feminist writings over the years she may have wanted us to think it was 'she, she, she' but really it was as much about 'me, me, me'. She would, say, grab hold of a theory that would make some money and harvest her some public attention. A few years later she might discard that theory in favour of, quite possibly, a seemingly contradictory theory. More controversy, more attention and money. In *The Female Eunuch* she attacked children as an encumbrance. Not too many years later she thought they were a great thing. First she espoused sexual liberation. Later she appeared to disown it. Make your mind up, honey! But heck, it was all good for sales and you have to admit that she knows how to bash out a bestseller. Any freelance writer is tempted to admire the old sausage for her chutzpah. It's just a pity so many trusting souls swallowed her words as gospel.

One of the best plays to come to the West End of London last year was Joanna Murray-Smith's *The Female of the Species*, a satire about a gobby, ageing feminist polemicist called Margot Mason (described in the dramatis personae as 'sixty-ish, handsome, impressive, a monster' – remind you of anyone?). Playwright Murray-Smith insisted that the character was fictitious but some theatregoers detected echoes of Miss Greer. In the play Margot says: 'Darling, there's nothing like a hefty mortgage on an Umbrian hideaway to help you find one more publishable thought.' Not that Miss Greer has an Umbrian hideaway. Tuscany, please.

Amid her ceaseless, saleable caterwauling, Germaine Greer pushed an idea of women's rights as being non-negotiable. Thanks to her long eyelashes and tanned Aussie bod, militant equality became glamorous. The paradox (of which this shrewd hackette was all too aware) was that she might not have been given a fraction of the attention if she had not been so jolly pretty. There was an arrogance to her sermonising, a privileged blindness to the fact that gender liberation might be great and amusing and intellectually stimulating for a university graduate such as herself, but was less practicable for poorer, less cerebral women. What about the low-paid shopgirl who followed Miss Greer's creed, bedded numerous men and then found herself up the spout and shunned in her provincial town as the local 'bicycle'? Was she better off as a result of her behaviour? A working-class girl does not have the luxury of moving easily to another job in another city, as more prosperous women do. The teenager who gives birth to a couple of bastards may be thrilled to know that Miss Greer (herself childless) approves of her right to have babies young. That, however, does not pay the nappy bills or improve her chances of rearing well-balanced offspring.

The state produced an answer to this quandary. It changed benefit rules to make it advantageous to be a single mother. In terms of individual happiness and children's welfare this was unwise, but feminist orthodoxy was more important than common sense. The public housing privileges accorded to single mothers are bog-standard madness, unfairness committed in the name of equality. Two-parent families – come on, let's be outrageous and call them 'normal families' – are discriminated against. They see the single mothers queue-barge them on the waiting list for subsidised accommodation. What do they think? Naturally, they think, 'Well, if that's what happens when you have a child out of wedlock, why bother with marriage?' And so the institution of marriage, which has done more than anything over the centuries to glue society together, is weakened. Equality freaks hate marriage. All that 'love, honour and obey' stuff shivers their timbers. Yet married couples stay together longer, produce stabler children and generally have a kinder, happier time than their cohabiting counterparts. Marriage is great. The Left's attitude to it is crazily destructive, harming its own constituents more than anyone else.

Germaine Greer may have made equality her specialist subject but she was too extraordinary a creature to have a realistic view of it. She was given house room by newspapers and broadcasters because she was 'good copy', not because she was wise or right. How different things might have been if she had become a mother. But she was that rare bird (dangerous word), a sexual nomad, in sway to the new, her own experience of marriage being a three-week dalliance – and even during that she managed to be unfaithful. This woman should never have been a sherpa to public policy. She was – is – a freak. An interesting freak, I grant you. But still a freak.

In *The Female of the Species*, feminist author Margot reacts with derision when asked about the impact of her teachings on less privileged women. She says, 'My dear girl, I am not a life coach, I'm a provocateur.' She adds: 'I can't be held accountable for the actions of women who happened to be impressionable at the very time I happened to be vocal.'

Perhaps the stage character of Margot, like Germaine Greer, would be relaxed about teenage pregnancy rates. Britain has one of the highest in the world, some 50 per cent of which lead to abortions. We Brits are also in the world premier league when it comes to sexually transmitted diseases among the young. The equality brigade has a stock reply to this: more sex education in primary schools! The more this is tried, the worse the problem becomes. The one thing they have not tried is questioning the orthodoxies of feminism. Might not the unhappiness and social disruption of so many teenage pregnancies be linked to the promiscuous hedonism preached since the 1960s by the likes of Germaine Greer?

A Cox and Ball Story

The 'Ladette' sounds like a Vauxhall mini-van from the 1970s. If only. The ladette probably used to be called a tomboy, as in George Kirrin from Enid Blyton's 'Famous Five' books. Not that the ladette would have had much in common with George. Young George (née Georgina) did not much like being a girl but she had as little time for boys as she did for pretty things. The ladette is keenly aware of her gender and sexuality and loves to dress in miniskirts, trailing the scent of alcopops. George was an outdoor sort of person, seldom happier than when roughing it in rain or caves and talking to her dog Timmy over a plastic beaker of lemonade (what a loser!).

The ladette is ill-suited to the outdoors, unless it be the pavement outside some provincial nightclub. She has little idea of how to talk to an animal, being too caught up in her own tiny sphere. And yet the ladette is tomboyishly masculine in the way she poisons her body with alcohol and mistreats it generally.

Sadly, no one told the Almighty that ladettes are equal. Women's bodies are biologically less capable of coping with alcohol. Ladettes try to disprove this, with sorry results. The first prominent ladettes included two BBC presenters, Zoë Ball and Sara Cox. Brash, blousy, bingeing characters, they showed off their appetites with abandon, and were greatly encouraged by the national broadcasting corporation. BBC managers felt under pressure to be part of the 'Cool Britannia' which was used by New Labour as a political rebranding exercise for our kingdom. Cultural neophilia created a slipstream for political change. If the idea of "the new" could be cemented as sexy, life for New Labour's legislative revolutionaries would become easier. That was the political-cultural mood of the time.

Miladies Cox and Ball had loud voices. Many feminists in the 1970s (apart from Miss Greer) dressed like whiskery dugongs but Sara and Zoë wore sassy clothes, always happy to bare an inch of flesh while swearing like building workers. It was all about an image of equal, rough-living, blokeish womanhood forging ahead in a new world.

How true was this image? Sara Cox, whose mother worked in Conservative clubs, disputes some versions of her childhood. One newspaper said that she had a comfy existence complete with private piano lessons and a pony called Gus which she exercised on her father's forty-acre farm near Bolton. She herself has claimed, in her harshest Bolton accent, a less enviable existence. She has said that her divorced mother had to take multiple jobs to feed the family and that her stepfather was unemployed for three years in the 1980s. As childhoods go it was, she proclaims, 'really hardcore'. Any reports that she is middle-class really 'pissed over the memory' of how it was. Ah, the argot of the modern BBC presenter. Peter Hobday never spoke like this, did he? But that's why he's toast and why the vocal stinging nettle of Miss Cox is all the rage. It's called reaching down. Being 'accessible'.

Miss Cox may seem determined to slough off privilege. Radiating ennui – she is one of those successful people who affects exhaustion, frequently claiming to be 'not quite with it' after a late night – she has had some notorious lapses of taste in front of BBC microphones. There was the time she handed over to fellow DJ Simon Mayo, saying, 'How's your penis, then?' (Shortly before, she had been discussing another presenter, Jamie Theakston, and wondering about the dimensions of his manhood.) There was the time she regaled listeners with her decision to urinate in her shower that morning. She allowed Ali G to bang on about the size of his own 'weldin' torch' and use the word 'motherf***er'. All on Radio 1, a public subscription station listened to by children and young adults. When that sort of bilge is being broadcast on the national airwaves we can hardly claim to be surprised when aggressive youngsters eff and blind. Time and again Miss Cox escaped with nothing more than a mild reprimand by Radio 1's controller, Andy Parfitt. This was the sort of low-grade sleaze which allowed Russell Brand and Jonathan Ross to think they could get away with anything. Ageing groover Parfitt's reward? Repeated promotions.

Sara Cox loves to put it about that she is a wild drinker, going into riffs about how at a pop festival she fills the jacuzzi of her Winnebago with gin, or in a BBC educational video boasting about how, after receiving her exam results as a schoolgirl, she 'went down the pub' to celebrate. Well, maybe. But maybe not. There is something calculating about her wildness, a sense that maybe it is a career move, a sales pitch, an effort to appear hard-nosed instead of behaving more gently, as we might expect of someone in her mid-thirties.

Sara Cox first arrived as co-presenter of a short-lived television programme called *The Girlie Show* on Channel 4, a 'post-pub' entertainment which meant oafishness was encouraged. It had lamentably low standards of presentation. It was one of those programmes in which the presenters make no effort to speak in complete sentences or give listeners an impression they know what they are talking about. *The Girlie Show* had a section called 'Wanker of the Week'. The show's producer could surely have qualified for this title every time. The programme flowed from the same gutter that brought us efforts such as *The Big Breakfast* and Chris Evans's *TFI Friday* – the same, ostentatiously drunken Chris Evans who has now been given a privileged berth at BBC Radio 2.

'Coxy' fancies herself a comedienne, the sort of wit who thinks it priceless if she goes on BBC Radio 1 and says on the day of the late Queen Mother's birthday that she 'smells of wee'. Charming. When ratings for her Radio 1 Breakfast Show fell, she larkily responded by saying: 'You do wonder where have they all gone. It'd been going up and up and then . . . I always hope it's a mass death among 16- to 24-year-olds. A good handful of car crashes and ecstasy deaths.' What a wit! Yet this is the same Sara Cox – who will unashamedly swear to a sympathetic newspaper interviewer and will boast in public about her breasts – who stood greatly on her own dignity when she was photographed nude with her new husband on their honeymoon. The photographs were taken by a sneaky paparazzo and when they were published in the *People* Cox felt that her privacy had been despoiled and her honeymoon ruined. She sued successfully and the photographs were destroyed. The newspaper had broken the rules of the Press Complaints Commission and it is hard to have much sympathy with its then editor, Neil Wallis. And yet, are we not allowed to feel similarly aggrieved at Sara Cox's own conduct on air? Can we not argue that *our* right to a certain level of decency, particularly from a national broadcaster, has been affronted? In the harsh, unthinking way the *People* behaved is there not a reflection of a society in which an obviously clever woman goofs about, talking down, glamorising crass behaviour and prattish humour, generally cavorting for low entertainment? Given the way she has conducted herself on air over the years, can we not sue her right back for demeaning our communal standards, if not of privacy then of basic self-esteem? All this from a woman who was given an honorary doctorate from somewhere called the University of Bolton for 'contributions to broadcasting'.

Zoë Ball was a more fragile sparrow than the gobby Sara Cox, and maybe a little more original but she offered a similarly poor example to her disciples. 'Kids' TV presenter Zoë', as she was called by the tabloids, promoted her career in children's entertainment by boasting about her drinking and her carousing. She bragged about her sexual come-ons – how she would wear 'full-on underwear' to tempt her husband – and how she liked to think of herself as a 'crazy lady'. When she married a drunken, pill-popping disc jockey called Norman Cook (aka 'Fatboy Slim', whose albums included one with the title *Better Living Through Chemistry*), she bragged to the world about how they had been given a 'sex swing' in their wedding presents. All this from a woman, as I say, who was the Valerie Singleton of her day. She was also the mother of a toddler son called Woody. One day poor little Woody will be old enough to read what his mother was saying about her wild life. We must hope that, in a triumph of hope over statistics, he grows up to be like Saffy, the daughter in TV's *Absolutely Fabulous*, who is far more adult than her mother.

Cox and Ball were promoted ruthlessly, by their own managements, by their producers and by the Left in general, as daring ground-breakers. Other performers saw that this was the way to make money. Charlotte Church, the child singer with a lovely voice, transformed herself into a cavorting hoglet, wrapping her tuneful lips round bottle tops as she eyed up the lads. The voice of an angel, the thirst of a tramp. The newspapers splashed her all over their pages and the girls of south Wales considered her their role model, to be placed alongside Zoë Ball and Sara Cox in the pantheon of modern women.

When these youngsters aped their behaviour, blokes thought 'phwoarr, wouldn't mind a bit of that' – and duly pounced. Responsible feminism argued for years that men should show more respect to women and should wait for the green light. Ladettes had the green light on all the time, as though they were ready at that very moment to rip off their weeds and start bonking like Shakespeare's country copulatives.

Jaded Generation

Poor Jade Goody, rest her soul, had little discernible talent. And so she became a pin-up for modern Britain. Miss Goody was the big-boned, pitifully ill-educated dental nurse who plugged herself in to the celebrity mains supply by going on Channel 4's *Big Brother* in 2002. She was duly fried alive by the media, to the point that even her early death of cervical cancer at the age of twenty-eight became a gawp-in for millions of lip-licking onlookers.

'Everyone' called her Jade, just as 'everyone' claimed to love her (save for those who 'hated' her with equal ferocity). Such is the familiarising, cannibalising, dehumanising process of television. Viewers see someone perform a role in front of the cameras. They assume that, as a consequence of that person having danced in the bright lights, they can claim intimacy with the performer's innermost feelings. This is a more corrupting rupture of privacy than any slight suffered by politicians and their powerful friends at the hands of newspaper journalists who have investigated how they spend public money. It is more cheapening of our culture. Yet we do not hear many politicians complain about it.

When Miss Goody died she was hailed by maudlin fans as 'a real person, just like us, unspoilt by the money'. This was not quite true. The reason Jade Goody made such big news for eight years, and so much money, was that she represented the lowest, the worst, the most stupid. It was her very dimness that interested the media and made her handlers a fortune into the bargain. Most of us are brighter than she was, though it might not necessarily stay that way if TV schedulers have their way.

Argentina had Eva Peron. France had Edith Piaf. The United States had Marilyn Monroe. We had Jade Goody. Only in a country with a bizarre sense of values, a country so terrified of excellence, could such a simple soul have become a pin-up, a doomed heroine, a melancholy totem of merit. Jade had no recognisable artistic or rhetorical gifts. To be brutal, she had a porcine face and, like your author, ran rather easily to fat. She was infamously thick, thinking that 'East Angular', as she called East Anglia, was 'abroad'. She and her supporters and boosters saw no shame in this dimness. It was even celebrated in one of the enormous floral wreaths which decorated her funeral. Her lack of intellect was paraded with pride. It showed that she was from the bottom of the pile. She was the duncing queen.

Her funeral was described as a 'public event' as though this was unusual. In fact all church funerals are public, just as all church weddings are public. The very idea of church is public. But should other aspects of Jade Goody's demise have been made so public? Was it necessary for us to be told the text of the 'last letter' she had written her two young sons? If, that is, she wrote it. It was an uncharacteristically grammatical document, not unaffecting. But was it truly penned by her or by her public relations adviser Max Clifford? Ah, the revolting Clifford. Here is the rat in the woodpile. It was this veteran sleaze-broker who seized hold of Jade Goody's career after she was told had cancer and used her cancer to 'revive her career'. Great news. You're dyin', girl. This'll be the makin' of you.

The media's ululations over Jade Goody's death were sickening. Only a few months earlier she had been disowned after a miscalculation in *Big Brother* when she was rude about (all bow down and face east) Shilpa Shetty. At that point in the confected cycle of public emotion, Miss Goody was still a baddie. She was the embodiment of the saloon-bar slag. Tabloid Britain attacked her. This vehemence was as false as the 'love' it would feel for her a few months later when her luck expired. In bog-standard Britain there is no room for shading, for moderation, for more than one side of a story. Feelings have to be driven past the limit of their existence. The 'bad' Jade Goody was no more hateable than the good version of the same young woman was loveable. She always looked to me like a sorry soul who was out of control. But the moment she was told, in front of a running television camera, that she was seriously ill with cancer, the bazooka of public opinion had to be recalibrated. And so began another grotesque transformation. What sort of sicko actually keeps the camera running at such a moment?

Jade Goody was trundling through life when she was picked up by *Big Brother*. She had the heart and lungs of an ox with an IQ to match. Television's bespectacled Berties were thrilled by this untamed creature. They had never met anything like her. They gazed on her as Kafka imagined anthropologists staring at a partly humanised ape. Jade was a grunting hog, a tusked sow straight out of the forest. She knew no self-restraint. She was, from that point to her death, the cash generator for profiteers who projected her as a symbol of egalitarianism. Richard Desmond's *OK!* magazine paid £700,000 to report her near-death wedding to a jailbird. Channel 4 made pots of gold from the ratings. Goody gumdrops.

Max Clifford argued that publicity was the only thing that gave Jade Goody a sense of purpose. Some of the money raised from the spectacle of her death would help to school her sons. Miss Goody lived for the media, by the media. But should we not have worried about the damage this case did to us? Jade Goody's well-being was not the only concern. There was also the effect the story had on our values – the triumph of unintelligence over culture.

Brown in Town

Maybe it was a Chairman Mao thing but Gordon Brown used to refuse to change out of uniform. You will recall that Mao had his distinctive outfit: a funny little suit with a bell-boy collar and high-heeled booties. That odd chap who has run North Korea recently went in for much the same thing and looked not entirely unlike Gary Glitter. Winston Churchill was another who indulged in political costume, his being a siren suit and floppy hat. For Mr Brown it was a plain, dark suit, a white shirt and red tie. When he was Chancellor he seldom wore anything else in public. Rumour had it that his wardrobe contained several identical outfits. We must certainly hope this was the case and that he was not simply wearing the same clothes day in, day out. Pong-eroo.

Mr Brown's clothes were an exercise in ostentatious egalitarianism. 'I'm Gordon Brown and I dooon't wear posh clothes.' This was particularly evident at official dinners. Mr Brown's predecessors, who had included far more obviously working-class men, never baulked at donning glad rags for the Lord Mayor of London's banquet. Mr Brown refused. He still turned up – hungry if not for the slap-up dinner, then for the acclaim – but he would not wear black or white tie. The Lord Mayor was not the only person to be thus insulted. Others who invited Mr Brown to a gala dinner knew that the brute boor would turn up in his grubby day clothes, not always radiating the freshest odours. Only when Mr Brown became Prime Minister and had achieved his long-smouldering aim did he relent and follow the dress code. Principle plainly was not the issue here. It was simply a tactic to help him reach No. 10.

Here was anti-snobbery at its flimsiest. No one would seriously have thought worse of him for putting on a clean shirt and dickie bow. His working-class clansmen in Fifeshire would have delighted to see their MP look smart in all the finery of central London. He was representing them and they, if given the chance, would have loved to dress up for such a do. Why should Mr Brown not look his best? Michael Foot had discovered the dangers of drabness when he was Labour leader and appeared at the Remembrance Day ceremony at the Cenotaph wearing an informal coat – a 'donkey jacket' said Tory newspapers. It is surprising that Mr Brown did not learn from that incident. Yet dour, difficult, class-playing Gordon insisted on pretending to be Mr Prole. In this respect he was a natural successor to Harold Wilson, who smoked a cigar in private but in public used a more down-to-earth pipe.

Mr Brown was not alone in dressing down. David Cameron has discarded the Conservative Party's old dress codes. Mr Cameron's John the Baptist in this was Francis Maude, an ardent moderniser who was the first Tory MP regularly to be seen on television without a tie. Mr Cameron took up the campaign, frequently wearing an open-necked shirt. The old custom of Tory balls being bow-tied affairs was scrapped. In his early days as leader, Mr Cameron was careful to have himself photographed at a Tory ball wearing a dinner jacket but no tie. He was trying to 'detox' the Conservatives' reputation for stuffiness. It was certainly a new look for them – and in that sense a shrewd political move, change being essential to political image. But how would you feel if you threw a black-tie charity dance and men turned up at the start of the evening without ties round their necks? Miffed, I suspect. This sartorial demotic sent out the message that we need not try our best.

Soon, even the word 'ball' was removed, the Tories' Black and White Ball making way in February 2009 for the Black and White Party. It was thought 'ball' might be too elitist. Press photographers were banned from the event and Mr Cameron was snapped only in standard shirt and tie – a rather Gordon Brownish red tie, in fact – in the back of a speeding car. It was the furtive sort of snapshot the press used to take of ministers dashing away from an airport after being caught holidaying with an illicit lover.

Why so sensitive? It was because his enemies in politics and the media have long attacked Mr Cameron and Co. for being children of privilege – and the charge damaged him. His education at Eton was brought up repeatedly when he ran for the party leadership against state-educated David Davis. His membership of the Bullingdon Club at Oxford kept being mentioned in dark tones, as though he had belonged to some Oxford branch of the Hitler Youth. Friends of Mr Cameron were so concerned that they tried to suppress a photograph of him in his undergraduate hell-raising finery. Absurd? Or a realistic appraisal of the damage such a photograph can do in a twenty-first-century Britain still paralysed by aristophobia?

The general rule in recent years has been 'the more privileged they are, the more reluctant they are to dress smartly'. Our elite has taken its cue from the billionaires of America's ostensibly democratic computer business, a business which is in fact incredibly elitist, being controlled by a small handful of geeks who speak a language few others can comprehend. City bankers, while happy to be paid seven-figure bonuses, make showy efforts to wear 'ordinary' clothes. This is why the City's old dress code of pinstriped suits has disappeared. The new way has been falsely presented as evidence of a 'more relaxed culture'. It is in truth *less* relaxed, the informality of liquid lunches having been replaced by tense, jaw-clenched back-watching and careerist plotting, all of it horribly sober. One orthodoxy – the furled brolly and the bowler hat, as imagined by the foreign caricaturists mentioned at the start of this section – has simply been ousted by another, this time of dress-down Fridays where almost everyone wears stone-washed denims, Ralph Lauren shirts and tasselled loafers. The new outfits are no less expensive than the old (Mr Lauren charges a good deal of money for his logo-stamped shirts). All that has been lost is the distinctive Britishness.

If people really want to wear baseball caps and deck shoes and Nehru collars and so forth, well, let 'em. The one time we are justified in protesting is when an informally dressed person turns up at an occasion where others have made an effort. You have taken your beloved out to dinner. You have chosen a formal restaurant. Everyone else in the dining room is in smart clothes. You sit down and are about to raise a Kir Royale to your lips when the neighbouring table's diners arrive – and they are in shellsuits. Morale takes some repairing after such a scene. Perhaps it is as well that handguns have been banned.

What would the workers who used to go on Whit marches in Manchester in the 1940s have made of today's informal dress codes? A friend of mine, publisher Terry Maher, used to dress up as a boy for the Whit marches. Terry's family was not rich but every year he would be given a new suit for the march. It was the done thing. Wearing that suit made young Terry feel special. Rich men who think scruffy clothes are somehow more democratic are simply being patronising. William and Harry Wales, take note. Young Terry Maher used to feel like a prince when his parents kitted him out all smart. Our leaders should do us the honour of dressing up to their station.

Title Deeds

Gossip columns are often knocked. They are considered fripperies on the outer precincts of the newspaper estate. As a former diary columnist I disagree. Diaries, or gossip columns, are not only one of society's most potent gauges of value but also rich seams for journalism.

Diaries examine the people we are being encouraged to view as an elite. It's like sizing up the runners and riders in the Grand National. They project an image of what we have become and of the social whirl. This is why people are so scared, yet envious, of diaries. They want to be mentioned in them yet they are also terrified of being attacked by them. To be criticised in front of millions of readers? Oh, the shame.

Fifty years ago the diary columns of the mid-market press concerned themselves chiefly with the activities of the titled aristocracy. Their marriages, successions and house sales were faithfully recorded, sometimes with a faint undertow of sarkiness. A system of court debutantes was still in operation to provide a splash of glamour – 'the Hon. Dora Twice-Knightly was presented at Buckingham Palace yesterday under the tender gaze of her parents, Lord and Lady Twice-Knightly and her raffish uncle Sir Reggie Nosebleed, known to friends as "Gloria".' Princess Margaret also did her bit for Fleet Street circulation figures. God, she was beautiful. Remained so until late in life, too. At the State Opening of Parliament in 1997 she wore a champagne-coloured dress so elegant that, even from the vantage point of the press gallery a hundred yards away, you knew at once that she was royal. She carried herself with sublime confidence. Margaret was not ashamed of displaying her sense of superiority and she demanded a second look. She did not always conform to the principle of noblesse oblige but she certainly demanded respect for her royal blood. If you have to be a princess (and she had no choice in the matter) you might as well acquire a soupçon of hauteur. It is expected and the British public do not like to be disappointed. No wonder the diarists loved her.

Diary columns also used to report the shire hunt balls, the national committee of the Conservative Party, regimental dinners, a handful of charities (the Red Cross, Rotary, Lifeboats, occasionally VSO) and a smallish cast of senior artists. The new-fangled was indulged infrequently. Diarists placed a greater premium on accomplishment, on authors who had published more than one bestseller, on painters who had the letters RA after their names, on musicians who had played to a full Royal Albert Hall rather than a gathering of perhaps a hundred scrofulous twenty-year-olds in a north London pub. It should be admitted that quite often these columns, which also tended to contain an inconsequential paragraph from Westminster, could be shrivellingly dull. The late Bill Deedes, who filed most days to the *Daily Telegraph*'s 'Peterborough' column, shrewdly observed that the perfect diary item contained 'one fact, one generalisation and one very shlight inaccurashy', the idea of the 'inaccurashy' being that it might generate some letters which would reassure the editor that the column really was being read.

Two decades later, diary columns were a great deal livelier. They had discovered a less grovelling tone (*Private Eye*'s caustic gossip column was in fact called 'Grovel'), yet they still contained enough interest in the British elite to try to identify its movers. These columns were more political. They piddled in the turn-up of the Establishment yet did so while observing social niceties, getting titles right and observing the codes of the Season. Their reporters knew what to wear for Ascot. They knew their way round the boat sheds of Cowes. They were not overcome by timidity in the face of a viscount.

These columns not only concerned themselves with the quirks and characteristics of Members of Parliament, but also sank their fangs into literary disputes among the better young authors such as Martin Amis and Julian Barnes. They still took an interest in the old men of the arts yet they were marginally less reverential. Young aristos continued to have their activities chronicled by Nigel Dempster in the *Daily Mail* and Ross Benson in the *Daily Express*, and although these columns were not always helpful to their subjects, they were written without too much sneering. The glossies had social chronicles such as 'Jennifer's Diary' and 'Bystander'. *Country Life* pressed on with its 'Girl in Pearls' frontispiece. There were also the Court and Social columns of *The Times* and the *Daily Telegraph*, where the Royal Family's engagements were recorded, where birthdays of important people were noted, where births and forthcoming marriages and deaths ('hatches, matches and despatches') were announced and where personal advertisements were placed in code. 'Darling Booboo, your roses arrived, scent with love. Rendezvous Wed pm, normal suite? Piglet xxx.' That sort of thing. These columns gave one a sense of living in a rooted society, a place where the social and the political were linked, where county landowners and diocesan bishops and elected MPs and the managers of the great arts bodies were all part of a sprawling but somehow balanced and evolving body politic. Royalty was at the top of the pile but the lower layers were not that much less interesting.

Today's diary columns are different. They concern themselves primarily with 'celebrity', often with figures drawn from talent shows or randomly selected from the public in reality TV trials. Pop stars, sports stars and their crumpet, celebrity chefs, that sort of dross. Most coverage is London-based and some of the great professional bodies and institutions go unmentioned from year to year. The shires might as well not exist and the Church of England is regarded as another universe. This is crazy, simply on a journalistic level. There is plenty of material going begging. Instead diaries fill their columns with inconsequential blether about TV soap actresses and footballers' wives, sensing that these people are more 'accessible' for the general reader. If peers or knights ever are mentioned, the titles are often used incorrectly or left out. The lazy presumption is that honours do not matter and that only enemies of egalitarianism worry about them. In the drive for some misplaced idea of equality, newspapers have lost the notion of society. Young journalists need to wake up to the gradations of power.

The criticism of the old gossip columns was that they reported a world beyond the reach of most readers, an inegalitarian world. But the same can be said for the celebrity culture of today. Celebrities are often simply members of the public who got lucky, sometimes because they look good or because they have some interesting deficiency. At the same time, the court and social page of *The Times* has been downgraded and moved to the outer pages, while glossy magazines devote less space to balls attended by honking Sloanes – and more to ill-disguised publicity puffs for foreign-owned boutiques in Bond Street.

Diary columns used to scrutinise the people who took decisions and devised laws and ran our institutions. Now we have social coverage of TV presenters and the latest freaks in showbiz. The truly powerful are being left to their own devices. Bad idea.

Keep Your Hair On

First there was Yul Brynner, then there was Kojak. Now you walk down the street and almost every hundred yards you are confronted by a man with a shaved head. Skinhead alley.

Hairstyles have risen and fallen over the centuries. From archaeology and art history we conclude that the ancient Brits wore their hair long. The Norman invaders of 1066 went in for pudding-bowl cuts, as did Henry V (aka Laurence Olivier). Cromwell wore his hair to roughly the same length as Ozzy Osbourne and the Restoration fops could have been models for David Ginola. By the time of Prince Albert, shorter hair was the thing, followed by the short back and sides of Edwardian days. In the late 1960s we were back to beards and straggly locks, John Lennon leading the way with his Jesus look (excepting the spectacles and Japanese fancy woman) when he staged his bed-in in Amsterdam.

So much for hair fashion. The move, of late, has been to have no hair at all. British blokes – and this is a strangely British fashion, not followed by Americans or continentals – have been emerging from barber shops like golfballs. Above I mentioned Yul Brynner and Kojak but these two baldies may not have been the inspiration. It seems more likely they have been taking their lead from the Mitchell brothers in *EastEnders*.

The Mitchells swaggered into the BBC's main primetime soap opera in 1990. They soon became the programme's chief motor, their toughness – you could call it oikishness – setting the tone of the programme. A glassy-eyed nation plonked down in front of t'telly at the end of a day's grind and followed the Mitchells' thuggish adventures: their feuds, their jaw-clenching petulance, their surly joylessness, their roughness not only to one another but also to their women and their mother, their criminality, their swagger, their failure to emote and communicate and even talk. As role models go these two were a disaster. They were also baldies, shorn not only of their hair but of all sophistication.

Britain's men saw the Mitchells, saw them lauded and kowtowed to by the other characters in *EastEnders*, and thought, as in Punch and Judy, 'That's the way to do it!' The Mitchells were a raspberry against self-improvement. They had no concept of morality or sociability. They just selfishly did what they reckoned was going to make them a quick buck, even if it meant wrecking life for their family. Those hairstyles said it all. They were aggressively ugly. They were brazen. They were naked in their nastiness. Britain followed suit.

Would you trust a dentist who had chosen to go bald? Would you want your children treated by a doctor who had shaved his head? Personally, I would not. The only banker I can think of who has a shaved head is Adam Applegarth, who was chief executive of Northern Rock. And look what happened to him and his bank.

Part IV
Our Rulers

A One-man Metaphor

It was the genius of John Prescott – a phrase that is somehow hard to type – to become the flesh-and-blood epitome of class paranoia. Angry, malodorous, destructive Prescott would not have become Deputy Prime Minister in any other country.

He was not modern in his outlook or realistic in his predictions. He was a bottom-pinching grunt with a gut and a temper – and as such he represented a considerable section of the British population. Yet he would betray them, just as he betrayed his wife. He was appointed as a token animal. Tony Blair made Mr Prescott his deputy because he needed a totem of what he thought was the working class. Old Fettesian Blair himself was awash with class guilt. He agonised about his lack of proletarian authenticity. His decision to appoint the atrocious Prescott was in its way as clear an example as we could hope for of this book's thesis: that the British elite's self-mutilation over class has led to a trashing of excellence which in turn has done no good to those lower down the food chain.

There was little about Mr Prescott that was elevating. He was not much of a reader. Although he had studied at Oxford (an interlude which got him out of National Service) he did not show obvious interest in intellectual self-improvement. One never heard him talk about mercy or happiness. The only time we heard him utter the word 'beautiful' was his sneering reference to 'the beautiful people' of New Labour. His caricature was one of rapacious hunger, of selfish insistence, of resentment and partisan covetousness. 'Toffs' were his enemy and 'toffs' would pay. The hatred he showed such people was remarkable, quite out of kilter with any slight in his own life or indeed the lives of probably 99 per cent of voters. And yet a signficant part of the electorate warmed to the man. Why?

They thought he was on their side – mainly because they did not think other politicians were on their side. He did not speak quite like the others, for a start. No one spoke like Prescott! But he was more direct in his gist, even though his words came out like half-chewed chips. Public relations men could no more polish this politician than they could an elephant's rump. He was at least honest in his chumpishness. He owed his survival to the fact that the political system, for all its talk about 'equality' and 'fairness', remained the preserve of a small, distant elite. Mr Prescott was its tame chimp.

He spouted all this stuff about fox hunters and Etonians yet in his own life he was not averse to hoity-toity airs. Croquet at Dorneywood, his grace and favour mansion, was hardly the pastime of a street fighter. His house in Hull had crenelations. His non-parliamentary earnings ran well into six figures – enough to keep even the statuesque Pauline in hairspray for the rest of time. Mr Prescott, in a reflective moment, said that 'we're all middle-class now' but he, in fact, was ruling-class. He had a driver and state-paid limo. He had first-class air travel to foreign climes where he toured like a global magnifico. The man was a twenty-first-century pasha who helped 'his people' barely one jot.

VIPs – Very Irritating People

Purists argue that the twenty-first century did not get going until 1 January 2001. However, the party held at the Greenwich Dome on the evening of 31 December 1999 was seen by many as the end of the old millennium. The bold new age began in the best possible way – with a comic comeuppance for the VIP crowd.

The Dome, largely a New Labour conceit, invited numerous 'opinion formers' to its opening night. The poor Queen was dragged along to lock hands with Tony Blair and sing 'Auld Lang Syne' (a forced annual jollity which proper Englishmen anticipate all year with dread). The photographs of HM in a hot little hat that night, mouthing the words with distasteful precision, left us in little doubt as to what she thought of the event. At least she made it inside on time, though. Many of the designated Very Important People spent a large part of the evening in a queue.

Ha! This was beautiful. In bog-standard Britain the VIP area is a burgeoning atrocity. The grottier services become for the rest of us, the more we see 'VIP area – keep out' signs in public places, separated by a little spool of fake rope and stainless-steel bollards. Airports have separate rooms which they call 'executive lounges'. These are now the only places where the airline experience is not a living hell. Nightclubs have them, patrolled by bouncers with twenty-inch necks. Pop festivals are almost the worst. Glastonbury has built itself on an idea of socialist freedom, of equality under the rule of cool music, but there are few places with a more beefily enforced VIP zone, stewards being equipped with walkie talkies, tabards and sausage-dog waddles. There is even a VIP area at the Hay-on-Wye Literary Festival (sponsor: the *Guardian*). Hay's festivalgoers could not be more charming. They would never dream of being impolite to a celebrated author, yet the organisers lay on a special tent for 'VIPs' with its own lavs and coffee pots and deep-set sofas, where leftie pensuckers in crumpled linen suits can avoid having to mix with their public.

Back at the Dome that ill-fated night, scores of ministers, tycoons, broadcasters and newspaper executives had gone swanning along, in open-necked shirts, designer casual jackets, brandishing their special invitations. Jon Snow was there, as was the then editor of the Labour-appeasing *Times*. Jaunty Greg Dyke, the Labour donor who became BBC director-general, had made it, as had – darling! – Sir Trevor Nunn. Luvvies for Labour were out en masse, some of the most faultlessly liberal grandees of the land deigning to appear. 'We're VIPs,' said these metropolitan prefects of the Blair era. 'We're too important to buy tickets. We're expected, y'know.' Indeed they were. Today's ruling class prizes no one more dearly than those with the power to hurt it. If you hold a position of influence in the media you are courted. You are massaged by a thousand little compliments. Mind you, the moment you lose that position you are let go as carelessly as a dropping from a seagull's bottom.

A better country would select its VIPs from venerable truth tellers. It would cherish its outspoken backbench parliamentarians, its whistleblowers, its freedom campaigners, the parents of its war dead. But these people were not what the Dome's organisers wanted. It was the meeja and the PR swells who were placed on the pedestal and invited to attend. Power is what earns you the VIP badge in this country nowadays. And at the Dome, yippee, they received a beautiful bop on the nose when they had to *wait in a queue*.

Caterwauling ensued. Thundrous denunciations were published in the press. Internal inquiries were conducted. Apologies had to be issued by grovelling officials. The media agreed (some of us had come to this conclusion long before) that the Dome and its anti-intellectual exhibition was a flop. It never did recover. But on that one evening it fulfilled a precious function. It put firmly in place a rabble of self-preening vultures, junketeering friends of Peter Mandelson, the courtiers and cheerleaders of a down-dumbing elite who thought they might casually pocket another unearned favour and spend the biggest New Year's Eve for a thousand years networking in some godforsaken wind tunnel in Docklands.

A year later the Queen very sensibly spent her Hogmanay in Sandringham.

That'll Cost Ya

Michael O'Leary is the jet-propelled Dubliner who has helped make air travel a misery. You want to sit next to your child? It'll cost you. You want to travel with a certain type of bag? More money, please. You want to speak to a human being when you arrive at the airport? Cough up, buster.

Mr O'Leary's Ryanair has been the most relentless of the budget airlines and he has enjoyed himself taking on cheap air travel's critics. He calls them snobs. But is it not fast-talkin' Mikey who is the 'snob', at least in the way he uses the term? He is the one who created the skulking rivalry between priority boarders and the rest of us. Why pay an extra fistful of quidloons to clamber aboard his disagreeable aeroplane a minute or so early? I'd pay more to stay off the ruddy thing until the last moment.

Mr O'Leary is in some ways an adornment to the pantomime of public life. He has a quick turn of phrase and his insolence is fresh. It would be wrong, however, to say that he has been an unremitting boon. He has certainly helped people of modest means escape to the Costas and further-flung patches of Europe for a few pounds less than was once the case. His adherence to the cause of mass transportation to sunspots – skin cancer for all! – is without question. But amid the sales hype he has pranged the notion of service and wrenched us all downmarket. As a proselytiser of mediocrity he has few rivals.

Environmentalists accuse Mr O'Leary of causing noise and fuel pollution. They may be right. What worries me is that in the process he has contributed to an attitude of 'we'll only try our best if you show us the readies'. The menaces start when you try to book a Ryanair ticket on the internet. You start off thinking 'great, this is cheap' but with each click of the mouse, each progression up the stage of the booking process, you have to spend more to gain 'privileges' which were once a given. It may all be logical. It may be legal. When you hear Michael O'Leary describe it you may be lured into a heady delight that such temptations are now in the reach of the skintest. And yet when it comes to doing business with his outfit it feels avaricious. You find yourself drawn into a vortex of miserliness, starting to resent your family for nudging up the running total simply by existing. A fever of misanthropy sets in as you try to get to the next stage of the booking process without indulging your wife in another bag, or permitting your child to sit by a window. Human nature is not always pretty and the Ryanair booking process shows it with all its warts.

Once on board one of Comrade O'Leary's glorified buses, things turn nastier, from the sharp yellow plastic of the seat tops to the insistent, insincere voice trying to make you buy expensive goods. Sitting there, hating it, wishing the tape would break and that you could have some silence, you are tempted to think, 'What we need is a Michael O'Leary to cut through all this crud.' But of course this is O'Leary doing what he does. This is O'Leary land, the hard-sell souk, the claustrophobic flying cigar case where grot is the norm unless you slip the monster another few pieces of silver. We never felt this way about Freddie Laker. The sainted Sir Fred! We even fell for that dreadful man Branson. So why are we tempted to hate Michael O'Leary? It's because in saving us money he makes us feel mean, like a tourist haggling with a rickshaw wallah. In the history of mankind there have always been more arguments over small change than over lost fortunes. Ryanair is really no better than those 'budget brand' bottles of lurid pink hair conditioner on the shelves of some supermarkets. They seem like a good idea at the time of purchase but as the day of consumption approaches you start to wish you had paid more. High profits. Low aim.

Airlines used to be more expensive but they pampered us. Post-O'Leary, stewards hold out their palms, demanding money like *baksheesh* beggars before so much as handing you a glass of orange squash. There is even talk of making passengers stand up during flights and charging for the lavatories. Bog-standard? It won't even be that.

Charity Begins at Home

Our concept of charity has been stretched like a teenager's bubble gum. Charity activism is today not just about helping the needy. It is also a career choice. In the 1967 film, *The Graduate*, college graduate Benjamin (Dustin Hoffman) is asked what he intends to do with his life. Which realm of adult toil is it to be? The law? Accountancy? Aggregates? If the film were remade today, one of the professions dangled in front of Benjamin's reluctant nose would be 'charities'. Cause? Unimportant. Whatever is fashionable and gets you noticed. Whatever pays. Think of the prospects, Benjamin. One good grievance uncovered, one good media campaign and you could be made for life. Charities and their think-tank cousins have become a fast stream into political life. They are the training ground for equality's stormtroopers.

This is one of the paradoxes of the equality industry. It has created a cadre of expert prosecutors who have done very well for themselves yet who have little taint of misfortune on their own fingertips. Maddeningly for them, they have no genuine misfortune to call their own. They talk about suffering and lack of privilege but it is clear they themselves are members of a brahmin caste which has, within its reach, as many of life's juicy apricots as did Rome's purpled ancients. These spoilt specimens will, perhaps, have some vague physical connection to the cause they espouse. It helps if the person leading a black rights group is, well, just a teeny touch Afro. A women's equality group is preferably represented by someone at least biologically answerable to the name 'woman'. But these human trumpets of equality, these anguished attorneys of the allegedly suppressed, are part of what we used to call an officer class.

They are shrewd all right, alive to any insult, quick to see an opening which would give them the chance to accuse opponents of 'inappropriate' attitudes and whatever dread '-ism' applies (sexism, racism, fattism, etc.). They speak a tongue which is alien to most 'ordinary people' (as they call them), a language shorn of humour, elongated to include the adjectives and conditional clauses of the moment. A few thousand cleverclogs make a dandy living at the equality agencies, many of them state-subsidised, which beat their bongo drums for egalitarianism. But these people are no more underprivileged than the Raj memsahib sucking down a gimlet on some verandah in Ooty. They do better than the minorities they seek to represent. They accentuate inequality in order to pay their own salaries. Stressing society's misery is their raison d'être.

Think tanks, most of which claim charitable status, act in much the same way. London *heaves* with think tanks. They assemble outside the Palace of Westminster as real tanks from the Soviet Union once prowled the eastern side of the Iron Curtain. We have think tanks to the Left (Fabians, IPPR, Demos, Smith Institute), think tanks to the Right (Policy Exchange, Institute for Economic Affairs, Politeia, Social Affairs Unit) and think tanks which are either squidgily non-committal or become testy when you suggest they have a political bias (the Joseph Rowntree Foundation, King's Fund, Chatham House). Some think tanks are paint jobs of older, more rackety concerns, the way the British Motor Corporation would give cars a fresh badge to try to make them more appealing. Thus, the Institute of Ideas (don't ring them – you might interrupt some thinking) arose from the ashes of *Living Marxism* magazine. The Henley Centre, once thought an independent forecaster, is now owned by a big advertising agency. Think tanks provide refuge for politicians who have fallen off the ministerial carousel, that plausible waffler James Purnell taking over Demos within days of baling out of Gordon Brown's Government. Think tanks give sacked newspaper leader writers a lifeboat on which to float for a few more years. Think tanks satisfy the urgings of intellectuals too dreary or indolent or introspective to make it as front-line elected politicians or media show ponies. They are a vast umbrella for middling meddlers.

In Victorian and Edwardian days there were clubs and societies, such as the Reform Club or the Royal Society for the Prevention of Cruelty to Animals. 'Club' and 'Society' are not thought acceptable words these days, being too elevated, so these groupings of like-minded busybodies today call themselves 'Centres' or 'Foundations' or 'Institutes' because such titles have an air of modernity. The word 'Institute' does not really mean anything. You or I could set up a boozing club tomorrow and call it the Institute of Preprandial Snifters (henceforth to be referred to knowingly as 'the IPS'). You do not need to clear 'Institute' with anyone, as you do with, say, the word 'university' or the prefix 'Royal'. Yet somehow 'Institute' has a formal feeling. It sounds important, official, well-established, and that is just the way think tanks want to be.

Bluffing is a large part of the game. They organise 'day seminars' and 'business breakfasts' (urgh) and publish 'research documents' when really all they are doing is punting a political idea as far upfield as possible, like the schoolboy full-back applying his boot to a wet rugby ball. They send emails saying 'have you registered for our conference?' which means 'please, please, please come along to our lunchtime bore-athon, if only for ten minutes – we're desperately short on numbers'. They have 'fellows' and 'patrons' and 'vice-presidents', by which they mean 'supporters'. Many of their youthful employees are work-experience shavers straight out of college, working for little or no money. Westminster journalists, always desperate for stories, are so grateful when think tanks give them an early peek at some highly selective measure of public opinion that they refer to them in their opening paragraphs as 'the influential think tank'. Influential? Or ambitious? The two are not quite the same thing.

Think tanks are driven by egomania. They become vehicles for the political ambitions of their directors, fronts for sub-parliamentary legislation, self-selecting forums where dogma is disguised as dispassionate research even though it has often been bent as a gynaecologist's forefinger. Think tanks are factories of fomentation, undemocratic, unaccountable, their sources of funds seldom apparent. They pump out demands for 'action' and 'change' simply to keep themselves in business. When did you last hear a think tank issue a press release saying 'status quo seems best way of muddling through – gone home for rest of week'? All the time we have this impatient, self-serving clamour. All in the name of charity.

Mr Squeaker

Politicians should broadly represent the views of voters, as broken into constituencies. For that to be possible they should be allowed and even encouraged, in Parliament, to say what they like.

Not a bad idea, is it? We used to call it parliamentary democracy. Yet the current House of Commons is so timid that many views go unspoken. It started with capital punishment, moved to immigration and now affects matters as varied as grammar schools, gypsies and sex education. Chunks of public opinion go almost unwhispered. Those who do try to speak the public's view are tutted and tsssked and told 'sit down!', particularly on immigration.

MPs tell you they are leading rather than reflecting the public's opinions. This would be a respectable position if the disparity between governing and governed was not growing so fast. Personally, I approve of civil partnerships. When they were introduced, however, a large section of the electorate had its doubts. Those doubts were barely mentioned in the Commons because they were held to be 'homophobic'. Personally, I oppose the death penalty. A large part of the British electorate takes the other view. Seldom is it heard in the Commons. I happen to think pederasts should sometimes be permitted anonymity. Again, this view is not taken by millions of voters, yet seldom is their side heard in the Commons Chamber.

How often can this happen before the electorate starts to feel its Parliament is no longer upholding its duty? If you can work that out you may have the formula for revolution. We can surely agree that the suppression at Westminster of views that are widely held in the country is a strange matter, particularly when the few MPs who do voice those opinions are greeted with hisses and shouts of 'disgraceful'.

Our Parliament is led by the Commons and the Commons is chaired by – symbolised by – the Speaker. The current Speaker, John Bercow, is a choice example of what our Commons has become. This sometime Westminster lobbyist, whose early days were devoted to extra-parliamentary arm-bending, holds views sharply out of keeping with his electors. He scorns the system which carried him to Westminster. In short, he is an arrogant little strutter, embodiment of democratic drift.

Attack a man's character in bog-standard Britain and you will invariably find yourself accused of insulting his minority group. Mr Bercow's father was Jewish. Those of us who took a swipe at Mr Bercow were therefore criticised, for example by the *Daily Mail* writer Peter McKay and by Labour MP Diane Abbott, of being 'anti-Semitic'. Quite where this left Michael Howard MP, who is Jewish and holds a very dim view of Mr Bercow, one cannot say. The shrieks of 'anti-Semitism' had more to do with modern Britain's grievance culture. Pungent polemic is disliked because it unsettles the consensus. The egalitarians cannot accept that we pie-chuckers might sometimes single out a man simply on account of his personal shortcomings rather than for his ethnic background.

Speaker Bercow is an unconvincing personality whose professed views have veered from sharp Right to soapy Left.

Until the year 2000 or thereabouts he perched to the right of Lord Tebbit, having been a member of the Monday Club (a member of its repatriation committee, no less). The Buckingham Conservative Association, seeking a new candidate for its safe Tory seat, fell hungrily on this gauche figure. It had just parted company from its sitting MP, a languid centrist. Some Buckingham Conservatives were looking for someone with more snap in his celery. Mr Bercow, this apparent rightwinger, won the nomination. For much of his first parliament he delivered the goods but then, like certain tomatoes on the vine, he started to turn. He softened. Reddened. He began making interventions more helpful to the Labour side than to his Conservative colleagues. The change became noticeable particularly after he had lost favour with his party leadership and left the Opposition frontbench. When Tories were speaking, Mr Bercow would make sarcastic noises from a sedentary position. When Labour MPs were speaking he would nod and say 'hear hear'. He even went so far as to attack the new Tory leader, David Cameron, and praise the 'statesmanlike' Tony Blair.

Mr Bercow's new positions were not shared by many in his constituency, an ardently right-wing seat which is one of the last redoubts of grammar schools. It is possible that his conversion to the Left was genuine. Yet it is also possible that his move leftwards was a feint, a ruse, a gambit for personal ends. He has admitted that he thought for a long time about trying to become Speaker, so we should not discount the possibility that certain goals were in his mind when he started to 'make his journey'. He will have known that to become Speaker you need to have the support of MPs in the majority party. Was this why he set about courting new friends, writing little letters of personal congratulation to Labour MPs about their speeches on the floor of the House, ladling out little droplets of gravy with judicious application? A PR professional was at hand to offer advice.

How tribune Bercow's views changed! He no longer concentrated on fiscal rectitude and social conservatism. He started to preach on matters dear to urban Labour MPs' hearts – things such as all-female and all-black shortlists for parliamentary seats. In special educational needs he found an impeccably saintly cause to champion, a cause Tories might not instinctively prioritise but could not attack without sounding heartless. He took up the non-controversial cause of Burma. Oddly, we heard little from him about grammar schools, even though this was something his constituents might have expected him to support. And yet to have championed grammars might not have sat so comfortably with his friend Ed Balls, who in time became Schools Secretary. Mr Balls is a useful person to know if you are seeking Labour votes for your campaign to become Speaker.

According to the search engine of the *Hansard* website, Mr Bercow made his last parliamentary speech in defence of grammar schools on 20 October, 1999. My publisher's libel lawyer would doubtless prefer me not to call this a gutless betrayal of the good people of Buckingham but we can surely express disappointment that Mr Bercow was not able more frequently to catch his predecessor's eye and defend the educational system preferred by so many of his constituents. Buckingham Conservative Association could have intervened. It could have de-selected the strangely wonkish Bercow. God knows, it might even have been tempted to call in the men with white coats, given the strange emphasis of his oratory and the bizarre flourishes of photographic memory. That the association chose to do nothing says much for its patience. The trusting fools! At Westminster Mr Bercow's behaviour became ever more rum – he accepted a non-ministerial job from Gordon Brown – yet the delicate balance of politics, shifting one month to the Opposition, the next to the Government, meant that there was no desire to provoke a 'floor crossing' by a Conservative Member to the Labour side. Mr Bercow surfed the rapids brilliantly but it left a sour tang on many tongues.

By the time Mr Bercow announced his intention to seek election as Speaker – a move unsupported by most of the parliamentary Conservative Party, which hated him with rare intensity – it was too late for Buckingham Conservatives to disown their Member. He had suckered them. The Commons' Labour majority voted for Mr Bercow to spite the Tories. A few days later he expressed his joy to be shot of the Conservatives (a Speaker belongs to no party), boasting that he was 'historically and perhaps even legendarily independent-minded'. He calls himself a legend? That's modest. Legendarily ungrateful to the Tories of Buckingham, perhaps.

This one man, in that moment of his triumph, encapsulated the selfishness of our political elite. His ambition had succeeded at the expense of the principle of representation. That is what drives these people. That is why our Parliament is so despised.

Wock On, Sir Peter

One of the people John Bercow clambered over on his route to the Commons Speakership – indeed, clambered over him physically that day he was 'dragged to the Chair' – was Sir Peter Tapsell. Let me tell you briefly about him.

Peter Tapsell, born in 1930, entered the Commons in 1959 and had a parallel career in the City. He was a Eurosceptic long before the Thatcherites. He is knowledgeable about Africa, having been close to Kenneth Kaunda and an economic adviser to the Bank of Botswana. He fell out with Margaret Thatcher over her determined monetarism, in which matter he was probably proved right. He has held firm to his doubts about European Union, even when they were unfashionable. In this matter, too, he can be argued to have been correct. Holding his beliefs, declining to soften his siege-engine rhetorical manner, he has long occupied the backbenches. Sir Peter has trouble with the letter R and this makes him easy meat for some of us parliamentary sketchwriters. Yet we adore him for more than his fwuity wasp. We adore his bravery. His consistency. His sheer, bloody-minded, once distinctively British truthfulness.

When that twerp Bercow was making his plea for votes in the Speakership election debate, he mocked Sir Peter. He put on the voice of a cartoon Tory elder and repeated Sir Peter's confidential view to Mr Bercow, who had boldly telephoned to canvas his vote, that Bercow was a couple of decades too young to occupy the Chair. The Labour benches, many of whose Members are made to feel small by Sir Peter's grandeur and courage, lapped up Mr Bercow's mimickry. Sir Peter, listening to all this a few seats away, gave a blithe shrug.

Who emerged from this incident better? In terms of the result, why, Mr Bercow. He became Speaker. He seized the power he sought. The chitterlings of ephemeral glory were his. But it was honour that fell to Sir Peter – the honour of age and of wisdom. He has been mocked before for holding unmodish views. No doubt it will happen again. But he was spot-on about Mr Speaker Bercow. All hail Sir Peter the Rock. Or rather Sir Peter the Wock. Now that's what *I* call a parliamentarian.

In Harman's Way

Today's composer of nursery rhymes has a tricky time of things. Independent butchers and bakers are still just about in business, despite the supermarkets' worst efforts, but candlestick makers have bitten the dust. What do we have instead? Diversity advisers, race relations consultants, human rights lawyers, equality practitioners. Try finding a toddler-friendly rhyme for that lot.

These occupations are ballooning like weightlifters' hernias. In the old Soviet Union you could be arrested for resisting the idea of equality. Now the same could happen in Britain. In 2009 the egalitarians, knowing their tide could soon be on the ebb, pushed for a big prize: the Equality Bill. Here was an audacious attempt to criminalise opposition to the creed of minorities first. The Equality Bill permits the state to prosecute citizens who do not promote policies reducing 'socio-economic disadvantage'. Lenin himself would have been amazed. Here is dogma being sewn into the statute book.

The Bill's jargonised wording is unusually political. It intends to 'ban discrimination in the provision of goods' and 'fight discrimination in all its forms' – and yet it would permit bus passes for the elderly. The Bill's supporters, far from 'fighting discrimination in all its forms' are also in favour of all-female shortlists for parliamentary seats. 'Positive action' in favour of 'under-represented groups' is encouraged by the Bill. Do we not have some double standards in operation here? The word 'discrimination' is being used to mean 'discrimination of a certain kind'. Loose language in a law is not the mark of a free country.

Among other things, the Bill could make it illegal for insurance companies to refuse to sell insurance to old people on age grounds. Hang on. Is it not up to an insurer if he or she wants to do a deal with a customer? A driver of ninety may well be a hairier insurance proposition than a driver of fifty. My father, aged eighty-two, finds that he cannot buy insurance for skiing. I don't blame insurance companies one jot for refusing to take a gamble on my father's snowplough technique. It wasn't particularly good twenty years ago and his bones have hardly strengthened since then. There is probably someone out there who, for the right premium, would be prepared to take the bet of selling my father insurance for a burn down the red runs at Zermatt, but his age is a perfectly reasonable argument to give when denying him cover. Not in bog-standard Britain, though. Common sense *verboten*!

(Oops. *Verboten*? Am I stereotyping German attitudes? Be careful, Herr Letts. Be very, very careful. When Tory leader David Cameron put on the mildest German accent to mock the Government identity card zealotry – 'Vher are your papers?' he said in clipped Teutonic tones – a member of the audience told him off for using an 'inappropriate' voice. For God's sake don't try to make a joke in bog-standard Britain. The humour police will get you.)

Equality has become a political trump card, a shield against criticism. When Caroline Flint found her Cabinet ambitions frustrated she quit the Brown Government, accusing the Prime Minister of being a sexist. Was he really anti-woman? I doubt it.

Yet Ms Flint's charge was treated with seriousness. When Michael Martin received raspberries for his performance as Mr Bercow's predecessor in the Commons Chair, some purple-snouted blowhard called Lord Foulkes of Cumnock said the critics were motivated by sectarianism and anti-Scottishness. This was hogwash – on the cry-wolf basis, dangerous hogwash – but it was written up in lights. To give my favourite bone another gnaw, Speaker Bercow was defended by Culture Secretary Ben Bradshaw, who suggested that critics of Mr Squeaker were still furious he had changed his view and now supported gay rights. Oh come *off* it, Benjie! Bercow is a prize prat not because of the issues he has adopted but because of the way he seemed to proclaim them to oil his ambitions. We suspected him of acting not on principle but out of ego.

When politicians utter the word 'equality' their faces go all wonky. They wrench their cheeks and mouths and eyes into expressions of anguished concern. Their voices acquire a soapy timbre, like cartoon dawg Scooby Doo saying 'Scooby snack?' If in a tight spot politicians reach for the E word and say that despite their faults they have always been champions of diversity and equal rights (at this point they will insert the name of some particular minority to ensure a burst of cheap applause). We are plummeting into an ethnic grievance Hades and we may soon reach the stage, like America, where politicians trot from one minority lobby dinner to another to make yet another insincere speech pressing the requisite homage buttons.

Equality is the last refuge of the shyster, the loser, the professional plaintiff and leech. These people are semantic Houdinis, creating tangled knots of appropriate language, appropriate attitudes, appropriate practice before wriggling out of them with lithe legalese. Black police officers, some better at hunting grievances than burglars, proclaim their membership of the National Black Police Association and jump up and down so much that ministers agree to support the enterprise with state money. The association demands that the nation become colour-blind yet it, itself, is a colour-defined group. Or is it? A small-print rider states: 'The definition of "black" does not refer to skin colour.' Whaaaat? So why not call it the National Green Police Association?

Very occasionally Equality's proponents stab themselves in the foot with the garden fork. Gordon Brown, having started pushing the Equality Bill through Parliament, comes up with the dog-whistle idea of 'British houses for British families'. Only after he has uttered the words does an aide sidle up to the Prime Minister and quietly suggest that this policy may in fact be illegal under the Equality Bill. *Praaaang.*

Back at the National Black Police Association, too, there has been some chewing of lower lips. Might it be illegal to have a group restricted solely to black people (however you manage to designate 'black')? Better bash out some more small print. And so they serve up the paragraph: 'Everyone within policing is eligible to join the NBPA. There is no barrier to membership.' This is absurd. How many white coppers are going to want to join? Meanwhile, let's savour point 4.4 in its seventeen-page, thirteen-article constitution, referring to the election of National Executive Committee members: one vice president shall be female and one vice president shall be male. Why? What if no woman or no man wants to be vice president that year? Where does this leave people of no set gender? By god, this inequality game's tricky. The more you dig, the more you find. As with contemplation of infinity, it will eventually turn you mad. Equality, like the overgrown sow, will eventually squash her piglets to death and have to gobble up their breathless corpses.

And indeed, civil war has recently erupted at the Equality and Human Rights Commission, the quango which eats £70 million a year of our money. Its leader, Trevor Phillips, made a (rather good) speech questioning multi-culturalism. Perfidy! He was attacking the very root of his outfit's being. Equality practitioners went loopy-loo and demanded his instant dismissal.

Harriet Harman, the Labour deputy leader who has created her political career out of feminist grievances, asserts that 'prejudice has to be stamped out'. Stamp, stamp, stamp. It's Harriet's speciality and with her big flat feet she is one to be feared. But the recent election of British National Party figures to the European Parliament is evidence that the more we hector voters about tolerance, the less tolerant some of them may become. Stamping doesn't work. Establishment egalitarianism ceases to look like fair play and starts to look like organised favouritism. Good teachers know that the best way to help a vulnerable outsider to integrate in a school is to be seen to treat him like any other pupil. He then becomes one of the gang. If we took this attitude to minorities we might find the BNP vote dropping fast.

Uncle Tom Cobley and All

As the Equality Bill started to pass through Westminster, lobbyists swarmed like hornets. The Equality Bill Public Bill Committee received written evidence from the following: the Disabilities Charities Consortium, the Chartered Institute of Personnel and Development, the Alliance for Inclusive Education, Unison, Accord, Friends, Families and Travellers, Age Concern and Help the Aged, Young Equals, the Equality and Diversity Forum, the Equal Rights Trust, the Discrimination Law Association, the British Humanist Association, the Catholic Bishops Conference, End Violence Against Women, Support Transgenre Strasbourg, the Equality and Human Rights Commission, the Equality and Human Rights Commission Disability Committee, the Finance and Leasing Association, the Gender Identity Research and Education Society, the TUC, Carers UK, plus second helpings from the Disability Charities Consortium. Phew. In addition to all this bumf, the committee's first two sessions took oral evidence from assorted professional whingers and stirrers. These came from the Equality and Diversity Forum (again), the Equality and Human Rights Commission (again), the Tribunals Service, gay rights group Stonewall, Press for Change (transsexuals), the Runnymede Trust (ethnicity and cultural diversity), Race on the Agenda, and a trio of wimmin's groups, the Fawcett Society, Women's National Commission and Women Like Us. A former director of Stonewall was helping to draft the Bill, furthermore, and stared down from the committee table, stern and unyielding.

This is but the nosetip of the equality lobbying submarine, most of these groups having chief executives, press officers, legal officers, constitutions, ten-year plans, advertising budgets and parliamentary liaison strategies. So much activity, and so much of it subsidised by the taxpayer. Public Bill committee hearings normally attract smaller crowds than village cricket matches, but for the committee's first meeting the room was as packed as a Tube in rush hour. The session was largely hogged by John Wadham, legal supremo at the Equality and Human Rights Commission. He crouched low at the witness table and, speaking in an E. L. Wisty voice, soon bored the MPs into droopy-eyelidded submission.

Here was the equality crowd at the cockpit, pulling the political system's levers, taking over. The air filled with Wadham's lectures about his 'core mandates of race, women and gender, disability, sexual orientation, religion, belief and age'. He addressed the MPs as though he was the minister in charge of the proposal, closing his eyes as he spoke – shades of a priest at the communion altar – and ending his epic paragraphs with small tweaks of the neck. The only MP who cut through this appalling drivel was a Tory, John Penrose, a polite, soft-spoken bird who noted that the Bill would force public bodies to consider inequality. Did they not do so already? Was there, asked Mr Penrose, 'any evidence of public authorities that are not considering the issue of equality adequately?'

For the first – and only – time in the session, the garrulous Wadham stalled mid-air. He opened his mouth but out came no sound. He shut it, blinked, rotated his neck and tried again, with little more success, to find an answer. Rather worrying, really. If the professional equality lobby's most seamless spouter cannot easily produce evidence of any failure by British officialdom to consider equality issues, what is the point of the whole, shiny, expensive Equality Bill and the vast apparat of well-paid lobbyists who, like the prehistoric logrollers who took the rocks to Stonehenge, helped to heave the awful law to Westminster?

And yet the madness persists. In the past year a Speaker's Conference – a rare and mighty-sounding body – has been convened to consider ways of attracting a 'greater diversity of candidates' to the elected Chamber. The premise of this talking shop is that the electorate has returned an unsatisfactory mix of MPs. It has not shown sufficient wisdom in its selection. Voters got it wrong again. Just like they did in a couple of Irish referenda on Europe.

The Speaker's Conference deduced that political parties have not been giving the electorate the candidates it needs to make an acceptable choice. The conference, while taking evidence from a succession of minority rights advocates, discussed the merits of all-female and all-ethnic shortlists for parliamentary nomination selections. We are here entering controversial waters, Perkins. Strap on the goggles. Is it proper for members of a political establishment to dictate the type of people who might oust them? If this went ahead, could white men find themselves sometimes blocked from standing for parliament in a country where white men are a hefty part of the population? You and I might not mind too much about this, but some of our gruntier fellow countrymen might – and might then be lured to agitate for that man Griffin from the British Nationalists. And at what point does someone start to be 'BME' (black minority ethnic)? I have some Canadian and Irish blood. Does that make me ethnic? My wife has olive-coloured skin. Does she qualify as a different political grouping? A friend of mine is practically white but takes great interest in his West Indian heritage. Would his children be preferred over mine in a parliamentary nomination on the say of some rule from a Westminster committee? If we start fiddling round with these things, might we not provoke racists? Indeed, is it not an example of colour prejudice to suggest such shortlists? These are honourable doubts to have, tentative though one is about expressing them. Yet when we turn to the written evidence of the Speaker's Conference we find one member of that committee attacking such doubters as 'a faction that does not want to be persuaded of the merits of all-female and all-black shortlists, cannot engage intellectually with the issue and, frankly, is not interested in doing so but just in being abusive'. Who was this beacon of tolerance? Why, it was the MP for Buckingham, John Bercow, now Speaker of our House of Commons.

The Speaker's Conference, whose members were largely predisposed to one side of the argument, did not take evidence from the BNP. I did not hear it take evidence from anyone opposed to affirmative action. The equality crowd was demanding total adherence to its orthodoxy, ramming its views down Britain's gullet.

In its written evidence to the Speaker's Conference the Equality and Human Rights Commission said that parliamentary politics could 'learn from other professions'. But politics should not be a profession. It is a vocation, a duty. That word again. Parliamentary politics should be about barking up for constituents and representing their outlook at the same time as pursuing a thread of personal thought. If it becomes a 'profession' it becomes over-complicated by codes. It starts owing its loyalty not to constituents but to the profession. This is what has happened at Westminster. The whole edifice is crumbling like an oatcake.

Fiddlers on the Hoof

The political expenses scandal of May 2009 was reported with gusto by the *Daily Telegraph*. That newspaper stepped a long way outside the Establishment bubble to rip the lid off our rulers' dirty habits. The British public was grateful. We had long suspected this lot were at it but now we had the elite's dabs at the crime scene. They had been preaching equality while stealing from the taxpaying poor.

As the late tennis commentator Dan Maskell used to say when an ace went whistling down the centre line, 'It's a peach.'

Let us not bother with a prolonged rehash of the invented mortgages, the moat repairs, the 'flipping' of home designations to avoid tax. Let us leave to one side the horse manure, swimming pools and ludicrously greedy travel claims, save to say it was a pity no Conservative warhorse caught in the scandal had the juice in his withers to reply: 'I have long told voters about the waste and greed found in the public sector. I have now demonstrated the truth of my theories to my own satisfaction.'

Egalitarian posing was at the source of the expenses fiddle. For years governments felt they could not pay elected parliamentarians more than a middle-management wage. There was a dread of appearing 'out of touch with the people'. The same 'people' were perfectly happy to see footballers paid millions of pounds a year and for general practitioners and some school principals to pocket more than £120,000, yet MPs were kept to a thin gruel of £65,000. It was a lie. Secretly they were told they could cane their expenses. With generous allowances they topped up their money to take it to something approaching the rates paid to other leaders of the community. When the fiddle was finally exposed, pop went the bubble.

Potential politicians who might have made better MPs decided they could not afford to seek election to Parliament. Egalitarianism was poison to strong leadership. We should have paid them twice as much (in exchange for cutting their numbers by 200 and ministers by a third) and denied them the little jampots of expenses. Instead we quivered before equality's mob rule.

For MPs, the salary became but an opening bid in their pay negotiation – as it has for a swathe of managerial Britain. The salary itself is merely a downpayment on the deal, the first serve, the initial foray up to the buffet bar in one of those all-you-can-eat-for-£8.50 Chinese restaurants. You nail down the salary and then you set about furnishing yourself with perks. Housing, staff, clothes, food, transport, weekends away: all these are regularly claimed nowadays by the executive class, if not from the company and clients then from the Inland Revenue in the form of items claimable against tax. The money comes from us, the taxpayers or customers. In bog-standard Britain we are the runts of the litter.

Tax concessions may be dressed up as delicate adjustments which make the system fairer, but really they are forms of special pleading. In theory the most level tax regime would be a flat-tax system whose simplicity would make it cheap to operate. This is a non-starter politically. Just think of all the interest groups who would oppose it, not least the accountants. The more complicated the tax system, the more work they gain. The more complicated the tax system, furthermore, the greater the scope for avoidance and evasion. This country has gone from being a land of instinctive honesty to one where discreet chiselling is the norm. Spivs were hated in 1940s Britain. Now they run the show, doing dodgy deals, knowing a man who can, winking at the accountant, milking the system. When half your income is being seized by the state, you naturally become furtive. But you might have expected the leaders of the system to be more honest. You might have expected Alistair Darling, as Chancellor, not to dodge paying for his own stamp duty. You might have expected the new Speaker of the House of Commons – an edifice built on the notion of fair taxation – not to be a property 'flipper' who used parliamentary rules to avoid thousands of pounds in taxes.

Casual cheating has been normalised because our leaders have played the system like Yehudi Menuhin with his fiddle.

Parking Nightmare

L eaders must temper their own pleasures. The old British elite knew this. Restraint was the price you paid for your privileges. One failing of the Thatcher years was the incontinence of the brasher rich. They showed off too much. They did not show that restraint. They were ecstatic to be liberated from the ruinous tax rates of the Callaghan government but their vulgarity was self-destructive. The Bolly-popping City lads and the larky brats of Oxford's Bullingdon Club and their ilk made it harder for the country to accept the idea of deserved wealth. That notorious photograph of Oxford University's 'Buller' boys in the 1980s, striking lofty poses in their feasting suits and pushing forward their groins, shouts of unearned swag. No wonder it is such potent fuel for class warfare.

Restraint is not merely a fogeyish concept. It is vital to the maintenance of a sense of community – and, by extension, nationhood. Gloating by the haves is as divisive as envy by have-not agitators. Those of us who might describe ourselves as patriots with libertarian leanings therefore face a dilemma. We are drawn towards individualism – so much more interesting than corporatist socialism – and think that the celebration of success encourages the young to try their hardest. Yet naked triumphalism is unappealing and weakens the sovereign state. It can stoke bitterness and demoralise the poor. When you look at the young George Osborne and David Cameron and Boris Johnson in their Bullingdon Club finery it is hard to resist reaching for an imaginary guillotine lever. I suspect we feel this anger because the Bullingdon was such an ignoble cause. Had those young men been dressed up for something more excusable – a wedding, say – we would not mind so much. But a nobs' club which trashed Oxfordshire hotels? Yuck.

Leaderly discretion applies in company car parks, too. Hierarchy is not an absolute good. Rank has its drawbacks and that little car park plaque saying 'reserved' is one of them. There is something distinctly unBritish about reserved car park spaces. It irks our sense of fair play as keenly as the stereotype of the German tourist bagging sunbeds by the swimming pool. A car parking space which says 'Ambulances only' is fine, but one which says 'reserved for the chairman' is maddening – not least because the space is so often empty, the chairman being off on another of his golfing jollies.

Choice of car seldom has much to do with necessity. Like the Bullingdon Club, it generally comes down to self-indulgence. Clearly a family of six needs a bigger vehicle than a couple without children and a Welsh hill farmer needs a sturdier machine than a Fulham banker. Most of us, however, choose cars on style grounds. We want to look good. Correction. We want to look better than the neighbours. This is not wildly noble. Car swank is the commonest generator of envy in modern Britain, yet for some odd reason it escapes with the least censure. Materialism receives an inexplicably good press. The boss who wastes £80,000 of company money on a car – as all too many did in the recent boom years – is in truth a profligate fool whose extravagance is taking money out of the firm, money which might otherwise be spent on dividends for shareholders or pay rises for workers. A car half that price would be equally comfortable. Spending so much money on a boy's toy (female bosses seldom waste such sums on cars) is done simply for status. In bog-standard Britain this is tolerated, yet the parents who spend £80,000 of their own money on sending a child to private school – while probably driving round in a clapped-out Rover – are derided for being snobs.

Special tax arrangements exist for company cars. If you are talking about a car for a travelling salesman who spends much of his working life on the road there may be a justification for this. For the majority of company managers, however, it is just another little perk, another diddle subsidised by the labouring masses. Why should a chief executive who spends most of the time in an office be given a tax break for a company Lexus? It is not socialist to ask this question. It is a respectable right-wing position. Company car tax breaks are an extension of the big state. Without these tax breaks the Government could be able to charge the wider citizenry lower taxes.

This is not an argument against expensive cars per se. On a shallow level it is an argument against expensive cars bought via dubious tax perks on company tabs. But it is also an argument for tactful spending, for chief executives not to splash the cash around on themselves and make junior colleagues feel small in their Noddy-mobiles. Let's have some tact and modesty, please. That's the mark of a really classy elite.

Got Your Name Badge?

The whole hideous area of corporate entertaining, a blight since the late 1980s, has smudged the line between leisure and work. Great occasions such as the Lord's Test match, Royal Ascot and the Chelsea Flower Show have been hijacked by the corporate-jolly brigade, tipsy floaters who are little interested in the cricket or racing or blooms. Fewer tickets are therefore available for the use of real enthusiasts.

We used to observe a strict separation of work and play. It made work more serious and allowed home time to be more of a tonic. In post-Thatcherite Britain, professional relationships are seldom allowed to remain just that. There is this terrible urge to 'get to know one another'. Cue the company 'family day' and the 'bring your daughters to work' syndrome – an extension of the cheesy American habit of placing photographs of the family on your desk. Hoariest trick in the book. Look, here's a snapshot of my late grandmother in her wheelchair at the old folks' home. Now see if you can bear to sack me.

Executives feel pressure to attend weekend conferences in smart hotels, sometimes abroad. One of the most vigorous conference-going organisations is the National Health Service. A doctor friend of mine, two or three times a year, is whisked off with his wife to expenses-paid weekend conferences in cities such as Amsterdam and Bruges. My friend, an anaesthetist, says that he already knows most of the new material discussed at the meetings because he is an assiduous reader of his professional journals. Just think: if they only stopped spending money on such events they could charge the rest of us less.

The more time we spend at such work events, the less we spend with our children and in our parishes. Sunday arrives. Do we go to church or to the company golf day – arrive early for buck's fizz in the clubhouse? Church is quietly dropped. Further decline of communal worship. Further decline in a sense of community. Yet again the family goes neglected.

Corporate entertaining is done under the banner of 'team building' and 'motivation seminars', sticky, unBritish concepts run by fervently optimistic fellows who smell faintly of anti-perspirant and never seem to switch off their positive vibes. Once they would have been gymnasia managers or vitamin supplement salesmen. Now they are 'life coaches', spouting superlatives and breaking everything down into three-step approaches and improvement regimes and slogans lifted from back numbers of *Reader's Digest*. You know you are in trouble at these events when you are directed to a 'registration desk', are given an 'information pack' and the young woman behind the desk looks at you with a primary schoolmistress grin and asks, 'Got your name badge?'

Employees have their spare time stolen by their companies. They are told constantly that they must attend courses and sit exams and add qualifications to their name, as well as meeting dreary clients with windbag tendencies and paddling fingers. Every con artist in town now has membership of some form of professional body with its own 'code of conduct' and written constitution. Another annual dinner to attend, another sub-scription to pay, and all in the name of something they call 'networking' but which is more accurately described as keeping your nose an inch or two above water in the desperate struggle for survival.

For many of us the working day has expanded so that it is no longer a question of knocking off at 5 p.m. Few wage slaves nowadays return home for lunch, as they once did, and plenty of them fail to make it home for high tea, too. Efficiency! Industry! Harder work for lower wages! These are the cries of the bog-standardisers. No, no, we do it like this, not like that. Follow the template. Show no spark of originality. We sit at identikit work furniture, Swedish designed, ergonomically of the moment, in vast, regimented offices like an Ocado warehouse, offices which could have been mass-designed – and possibly were – on graph paper. These workplaces are no more uplifting than the huge loom-rooms of the nineteenth-century mills. Individualism is frowned upon and the only way to get ahead is to work ever more hours. The corporate destiny is pressed on us instead, so we are forced to surrender one night to the 'monthly office heroes award', and another to the departmental paint-balling expedition ('please bring training shoes and something for the wet t-shirt contest'). We have to cheer like ecstatic morons – that horrid, fake, Kansas whoop – when our workmates win some vulgar prize in the 'office oscars'. Sales gurus arrive to speak about 'goals' and 'success' and 'platinum clubs', while through the windows all we can see outside is the rain descending on another melancholy day in suburban, sodium street-lamped England. If they would only let work be work rather than some alternative life. Middle executives are expected to devote their entire being to the core task of slavish adherence to the corporation, even if it is only an oven parts supplier in Droitwich. And on it goes, demands draining our energy, robbing us of tranquillity, thieving our souls.

An absurd idea persists that we have made great strides in our civilisation, that we should be lucky to inhabit this paradise of equal Britain. Yet it is not obvious that the work we do today is any superior to that of a century ago. In certain areas of craftsmanship, the opposite is demonstrably the case. Meanwhile, our curiosity and self-respect is dimmed. Our sense of family is weakened. The notion of personal improvement, once linked by the admirable working-class Manchester Movement to intellectual stimulation, has been ousted by career advancement. When not 'chilling out' and 'relaxing' (euphemisms for sloth), we have been drilled to rotate the corporate treadmill. Public libraries, created by the philanthropic Victorians, are no longer about reading and quiet study. The focus is on 'information', the counters bedecked with leaflets and garish posters. Visit the local fun fayre. Avoid AIDS. Do Not Become a Victim of Ruddy Crime. A public library in Gloucestershire, God help us, recently started playing piped music to make visitors feel comfortable. 'Libraries are no longer about books,' said a spokesman. It is at such a point that the theatregoer watching *Hamlet* is tempted to say, 'Drink the poison, Gertude, and after you with that goblet.'

Seaside Folly

Today's rulers, having been brought up in the era of the Beatles, think of themselves as modernisers. They consider themselves open to change, liberal and groovy, yet most of them are snails, as slow to alter their ways as any previous end-of-era elite. One small example of this is the annual political party conference season in early autumn, an increasingly corrupt circus.

The TUC go first, then the Liberal Democrats, followed by Labour and the Conservatives. These political gatherings are, to put it mildly, strange events. Almost no formal conferring is done. Few decisions are entrusted to the volunteer activists. Such people may be allowed to attend in limited numbers, but hardly any of them speak from the platform. Very occasionally a person with a walking stick or a wall eye or a set of ill-fitting teeth does make it through the screening process and is permitted a three-minute gobbet before being tidied away. When this happens, the political professionals assume expressions of patronising amusement. Oh look, there's a 'real person'. Yet these same political professionals are the same ones who talk about 'empowerment' and 'bottom-up decisions'. Egalitarian waffle. Ask not what you can do for equality. Ask what it can do for you.

Party conferences make money. Outsiders pay big sums to attend. Lobbyists see a party conference pass as an investment. It allows them to cuddle up to politicians (sometimes literally) and buy influence. The centre of a conference nowadays is not the hall where the speeches are made. At night it is the bars, where fantastically heavy drinking is done. By day it is the exhibition hall where the corporations and trades unions and lobbyists and pressure groups set out their stalls, complete with free pens and product samples and public relations officers. This is not politics as a battle of ideas. It is politics as an exchange of business cards, politics as schmooze, provided you have the liver for a month of late-night swilling.

Attending all four conferences as a reporter, I see the same lobbyists, the same sales smoothies, at each party's gathering. At each one they contrive to look intimate, giving an air of quiet support. They buy politicians champagne at 3 a.m. as though they were the best of mates. But all they are after is a sale. If voters could witness the sluicing and swearing, the cynicism, the prosaic venality, the vapidity of the 'debates', they would be appalled.

By taking a stall at a conference, an organisation shows that it is in the swim. It is playing the game in which access to the elite is more important than strength of argument. Spot the rising stars, slip them a freebie or some paid 'work', and when they become ministers you will be well placed for cashback. Sponsor a fringe meeting and worm your way into politicians' affections. Personal face-time equals influence equals, well, corruption, I'd say.

This is an elite every bit as excluding as the pre-1960s Establishment, except that elitism now tries to disown high standards, fearing they are inegalitarian. To enter this elite you must learn certain codes. You must learn the language of non-judgementalism and adopt an expression of moist sincerity whenever a member of a minority is talking. You must nod dolefully when it is suggested that the Third World deserves subsidies. You must agree 'absolutely' (most overused of adverbs) with demands for an end to 'prejudice' without ever thinking things through from first principle and realising that prejudices can actually make people stimulating. Imagine a novel in which no character had any prejudice and you might as well shoot yourself.

Among many presumptions is the argument that strong political parties are essential to a modern western democracy. Are they? Weak political parties might be a better idea. The weaker a party's whips, the more likely it is that policies can be considered on the strength of the argument. Strong whips force bad MPs to pass laws as easily as water. There is some validity in the argument that political parties can keep extremism in check – a strong Opposition in 1930s Germany might have neutralised the Nazis – but too strong a party code prevents dissidents from having a view. The over-mighty party machine soon becomes detached from the electorate. Party conferences, far from being a connection with the mass membership of the movement, are part of this process of detachment.

So let's do away with party conferences. Let's scrap the stage-managed protestations of loyalty, the shutting down of dissent, the gruesome business of the leader's speech with its Nuremberg applause and dishonest video presentations and its Blairised language from which full stops have been eradicated. Political leaders would spend their time better if they stayed in their constituencies, talking to the electorate by day and in the evening doing some autumnal pottering in the garden. The sketchwriters could have a few extra weeks off, too.

Security Blanket

That Pope Benedict in the Vatican needs to get with it. Standing there with Swiss Guards all dolled up with harlequin pantaloons and glistening halberds. How inefficient. Same with the Queen at Buckingham Palace. Bearskins and six-foot-five-inch Guardsmen, indeed. If Her Majesty and His Holiness want to join the twenty-first century they should be guarded by a scrofulous little sniveller from Group 4, some lily-fingered, fluffy-chinned youth with a bad case of the wheezes, standing guard with his automatic security pass reader.

What a delicious thing 'security' is, one of the few growth industries of the past decade. For centuries our monarchs made do with a Beefeater's cry of 'Halt! who goes there?' Now that traditional shout has been replaced by halfwit Ryan or Debbie from some 'executive security' firm passing a hand over their spotty chin and saying, 'Can you turn over your lanyard so I can see your pass?'

The Americans went security-crazy long before we did. That unfortunate episode in Dallas in November 1963 was partly but not entirely to blame. 'Security' means jobs for the grunting heavies. When Barack Obama came to London a few months ago the home side's security detail went into such overdrive that fourteen brand-new Land-Rovers were parked in the court of the Foreign Office to make sure he came to no harm. It was almost as bad when Mrs Obama, minus her husband, came to London in early June 2009. She was ferried round the city in two enormous Chevrolets with body panels as thick as submarine doors. We would have been quite within our rights to say to the Americans, 'Calm down, dears, and you may find you make her less of a terrorist target.' But of course no one did. 'Security', see?

'Security' means having the right to stop innocent civilians and conduct body searches. 'Security' means employing blokes who would be lucky to get a job peeling spuds in a fish and chip shop and giving them the power to obstruct and intrude and satisfy their petty authoritarian urges. 'Security' is really about proving your own importance by making life difficult for other people. A gun-toting motorcade is the ultimate in one-upmanship. When the Prime Minister gives evidence to the elders of the parliamentary liaison committee and has his bodyguard sit behind him, gun discernible in his bulging jacket, it is not so much because he fears his life is under threat but because he wants to show the MPs how important he is.

Security is now mad at party conferences, delegates sometimes queuing for an hour to gain admission. The voters are kept well out of the way, thank you, self-important goons striding about the place like black-macintoshed gauleiters. It is almost as bad at airports and government offices and even at some of our schools. Our leaders are so frightened of 'consequences' that they never question the right of departure terminal security personnel to hold out an admonishing hand and say, 'Take off your shoes and belts and walk through the metal detector.' Why? If the machine is too feeble to tell if I have a knife in my shoes, how can it be trusted to check my Y-fronts for a hidden grenade?

Is it vital for every four-year-old child to be subjected to this nonsense before getting on a flight to the Med? They dare not use their initiative and single out the genuine suspects because then they might be sued for discrimination. Excuse me, sir, I couldn't help noticing that you have a long, bushy beard, that you're sweating like a sponge and that you keep mumbling something about 'the Prophet'. Would you mind terribly if we just asked you a few questions? Who could complain about that? You want to say 'no one' but then you remember that we now have a no-win-no-fee law which permits solicitors to chase clients' cases on a speculative basis. We also inhabit a world where a British Airways employee was told she could not wear a tiny cross around her neck because it might 'cause offence'. Bog-standard Britain is so flattened by fear of prejudice that it runs up the white flag.

Politicians could mark a long-overdue revision of this security mania, this fixation that we are all about to be blown to smithereens by Al Qaeda (it used to be the IRA but they've now become cardigan-wearing grandfathers – even freedom fighters have retirement plans these days). They could say 'the millions of pounds of public money we spend on security is a farce'. But they will not do it because they relish being on the inside of a security cordon. It makes them feel big. The various levels of security pass – which zone are you? – bestow power to insiders. It is a life and death matter, or so we are told, and the people who issue the security advice are secret figures who can never be identified. What do we do? We swallow it. We accept. We have been beaten.

No Sugar, Please

No one should have expected Sir Alan Sugar to behave like a demure Edwardian spinster, but the manner of his joining, or not joining, the Government of Gordon Brown in June 2009 was a vignette of standards in British public life.

He could have been an adornment to our country. He created a computer business and made himself a fortune. Good for him. He overcame the occasional setback. On the face of it Sir Alan Sugar should be seen as a fine upstanding gent, albeit a scruffy one. The beard does make him look like a monkey with mange.

There is, however, a coarseness about this man which goes beyond the roughness of his beard. He seems so angry. Long before he was invited to front *The Apprentice* for BBC1, he would pop up on the television screen from time to time to offer the country the benefit of his experience. Such a cross little chap! Once he was on *The Apprentice* he soon confirmed early impressions. He relished his power. His language was unpleasant and he stabbed out his finger towards the camera, all chippy and show-offy. Was this really the only way to become successful? What happened to understatement? Where was courtesy and charm? Nah! Eff off outta here. Yer fired! Behave like a hooligan and watch the ratings rise. Thousands of would-be tycoons saw this behaviour and thought, 'That must be how you do it.' Well, it's one way, yes, but not the only way. Other people have become successful without being such tartars.

And then he had to go and join our Government as some sort of trade champion. He accepted a position from Gordon Brown and – frustratingly, we do not know the precise circumstances – received a peerage in the process. He had little notion of what this entailed. Asked if it would be a 'working peerage', he indicated that he did not understand the expression. He did not know what his job would be, precisely. And yet he would be keeping his *Apprentice* job, oh yes, you betcha. Give up some fame? You gotta be effing joking. Preen. Profane. Pout. Alan Sugar. Not sweet at all.

Short and Curlies

O ur political class has a horror of losing its perks. Nothing new. In 1970, soon after losing the general election, Harold Wilson was seen queuing for a taxi late one night outside the Members' Entrance to the Commons. Friends of Wilson were distraught. A few days earlier he had been Prime Minister but there he now was, waiting for a cab like the rest of humanity. Instead of seeing this, as they could have done, as eloquent testimony to the ephemeral nature of elected office, Harold's cronies secured him a state-paid limo and chauffeur.

We have been paying ever since for Leaders of the Opposition to be thus pampered. In 1974, having regained the premiership, Wilson returned the compliment by slipping the shadow cabinet a wad of public money. This 'Short money', named after Edward Short, the Labour minister who presented the proposal to Parliament, is now worth some £7 million a year to the Opposition parties. Short money was given on the premise that an Opposition would be improved by having researchers who could prepare meaningful policies. It would result in better government. Nice one! In practice, Short money allows an Opposition to save its money for election campaigning. This creates an arms race of electoral fundraising which in turn results in dodgy donors being given undue pre-eminence over the political parties' mass membership. Short money also allows Opposition spokesmen to keep large retinues which makes them feel important and saves them having to do so much thinking for themselves. Result: an overblown secretariat, lazy parliamentarians, hefty bills which have to be picked up by the taxpayer. Short money is an expensive con. All it has done is expand a professional political class. And all because socialist Harold's friends thought it was improper that he should have to queue for a taxi.

All Change

Bring back the bus conductor. It is four years since they disappeared from regular London bus routes. 'Clippies' brought a human dimension to public transport but were done in by petty penny-pinching and an accountancy idea of what makes sense.

One can over-romanticise the bus conductor. Some were cheery souls, swinging through the cabins of their Routemaster buses with their hip bags of spare change and their basso profundo chants of 'any more fares?' And that was just the female ones. As a child I was transfixed by the red stripe down their trouser legs and the metal dials and levers on their ticket dispensers. A turn of the handle and out came the ticket, forked like a lizard's tongue. 'Any more fares, please? Move right on down the bus.' Some conductors, however, could be astonishingly rude. The peevishness, the weariness, the way their truculence would increase with one imposition after another – such as the old £20 note for a 50p fare trick. Ha! It was like watching a pan of milk rush to the boil.

Conductors were theatre. They were a character study. They would help older passengers with their shopping bags and assist the young mothers with toddlers. If a pretty woman needed a steadying hand at her elbow (or somewhere else . . .), the conductor would be there in a trice. The lonely and the mad would find, in the conductor, somebody to talk to, somebody with whom to make some precious contact in a city where too often we barge past without a word. Out-of-town visitors could ask the conductor to let them know when to alight – 'next stop Hatchards book shop' – and foreigners could take the conductor's photograph and enquire the way to London Zoo. Conductors were among the last public employees to wear peaked caps.

The late Loelia Duchess of Westminster allegedly said that any man over thirty who used a bus was a failure – the quotation is sometimes wrongly attributed to Mrs Thatcher. Her Grace, not for the only time in her life perhaps, was wrong. In London the bus can be the most civilised of conveyances and it is the mark of a successful man, surely, to aim to be civilised. In summer a bus can be airy and comparatively cheap. Why sit in a limousine when you can zip by in a bus lane? Show me a stockbroker or a banker who takes the bus rather than wasting clients' money on a chauffeur and I will show him or her some of my custom.

Buses used to be fun. They had a buzz of humanity, conductor and driver creating a team. Now you just get the poor driver, lonely behind some security glass, leaning forward on the steering wheel while an automatic voice announces the next stop. Late at night, conductors made a bus feel safer. They could tell the drunks and bullies to stop being a nuisance. With conductors on board, each bus journey felt different. But then the cost controllers started to ask questions. Consultants were asked to do surveys. Ruddy consultants. One lot, the Boston Group, are known as 'The Boston Stranglers', such is their record for suffocating jobs. Once you have asked a consultant to do a survey the answer is a foregone conclusion: sack staff, particularly when stroppy trades unions are involved.

Who can say what other motives propelled transport bosses to exterminate bus conductors? Did salesmen from unknown agencies bribe fleet-buying middle-men to acquire new, conductor-free vehicles? One way or another, London spent a fortune getting rid of the conductors, scrapping the venerable Routemasters and buying hundreds of bendy buses. The whole thing was expensive but the bog-standardisers had their way. The London clippie had reached the end of the line.

The Routemaster was ancient by the time it disappeared. That it survived so long was testament to the public's love. The hop-on, hop-off platform allowed the bus to move away from each stop more quickly than driver-only buses. Passengers could alight when they wanted. Freedom. Choice. But health and safety wallahs and their collaborators in officialdom did not want that. Heavens, no. Give the customer what he wants? Ridiculous. And so they resorted to the customary ploys, the objections based on modernisation, equal opportunities grounds, things no longer being acceptable in this day and age. Routemasters were 'dangerous'. They were 'inaccessible to wheelchair users'. They 'created too much pollution'. They were 'too expensive to run owing to the conductors' wages'.

Dangerous? Well, only if the passengers behaved like idiots. If the law protects idiots and pays them compensation when they have hurt themselves, the law is itself idiotic. Tricky for wheelchair users? Can't argue with that. But how many wheelchair users actually *want* to use buses? Rather than altering buses to provide wheelchair access, could we not give disabled people some money for taxis? Routemasters certainly expelled a lot of exhaust but that was a result of their old engines and nothing to do with the design of their bodywork. And then there is the question of the conductors' wages. Well, reader, have you ever been on a bendy bus? How often have you seen passengers actually pay a fare? Put conductors on the minimum wage and offer them a percentage of fares raised – say 10 per cent – and I bet they'd make more money for the bus companies and for themselves. You would end up with energised conductors, happy passengers, lower unemployment, lower costs, quicker buses, chuffed bosses and a city which was much more fun.

Throughout public services we find this blindness of bureaucracy to the quality of the 'customer experience'. It is evident in the call centres whose subcontinental operatives seem to speak to you down a long wind tunnel. It is evident in the Post Office closures and the vast bonuses paid to Royal Mail executives. It is evident in the electricity and water companies which insist on giving you such impossibly long reference numbers that your eyes swim as you try to read them. Doctors' surgeries will not open on Saturdays and insist on not booking certain types of appointment more than a few hours in advance, rubbish collectors stroppily decline to take away your bins if they are an inch out of place, cinemas employ switchboards which are are operated by 'telephone trees', banks impose a heavy overdraft charge even though there is plenty of money in your feeder account, television companies make it as difficult as possible to lodge a complaint, government agencies will not connect you to the official who dealt with your case and British Telecom hirelings say, 'Your call has been lodged and will receive attention at the earliest opportunity – your business is important to us,' two weeks after you told the buggers that your line, on which you depend to earn your living, has gone phut.

Only in a country where the bog-standard has driven out the best, just as grey squirrels have driven out the reds, would this crapola be tolerated.

Warning: We're in Charge

That jar of breakfast Marmite, some canned peaches in the pantry, even the tube of Deep Heat embrocation in your bathroom cabinet: all have a little panel somewhere on their packaging, telling you to discard them by a certain date. Sell by, best by, use by – nag, nag, nag, from cradle to old people's home. Whatever the product, someone, somewhere, has taken the liberty of imposing a deadline on your digestive tract and consumer intentions. You there! This packet of lime jelly is three months out of date. Buck up! What an exhausting world we inhabit where even the date by which we must finish a packet of chocolate digestives is subject to official guidance. First they process our food, now they process our larder habits, right down to the curry powder and soy sauce. Can't they leave us to decide anything for ourselves?

The main cause of burst blood vessels in twenty-first-century Britain is no longer amateur weightlifting, unpressurised air travel or marital rows. It is the presumption of petty officialdom to create employment by devising regulations and control systems. Homogenise. Integrate. Standardise. Stipulate. In short, interfering ninnydom wants to corral and harry us down various behavioural tunnels like sheep farmers' collies on *One Man and His Dog*. They want us to know that they're in charge, they're on the inspection trail, laying down edicts, stating parameters. How else can we explain the desire to tell the buyer of a bag of table salt – salt, for God's sake, the great preserver – the date by which its last grain should have been gobbled? Eat up! The whole country will be staying behind until you have cleared your plate.

Nature has its rotting mechanisms. The shop-bought banana, particularly if left in near conversation with its zesty friend the orange, will start to acquire a mottled complexion. Soon it has more liver spots than the hands of a Daimler owner in Bournemouth. Later the banana turns so completely black it could be a body part from one of those Saxon corpses they dig up from time to time in the marshes of East Anglia. By and large, the British adult is capable of deducing that this blackening is a sign that the banana has strayed past its best. The egalitarian may operate on the basis that we are all idiots, but we are not. Cucumbers, once opened, are liable to curl in on themselves and become squidgy. After perhaps eight days, bin job. Less than completely fresh chicken will fill your fridge with a Neapolitan back alley pong. Bacon, like certain types of polyester trousering, will develop little bobbles of imperfection after a certain stage in its decomposition. As the Queen might say, this is its rind-about way of saying orf. We have these natural hints about what might not be such great scoff. Why do we not follow them? Mothers, before feeding babies, will tongue-test the food for temperature and taste. Even the most slovenly teenager has an instinct as to when a pot of coleslaw has become fizzy. So why do we need to have it spelt out on the packaging as to when something might be high?

The real game here is one of power, an officialdom which becomes queasy at the very notion of personal responsibility. Its members refuse to trust us lower orders to look after our own interests (militant egalitarians can be frightful snobs). They can only imagine a world in which everything is ordered according to some state-monitored unity.

Some of us happily ignore best-before warnings, chewing our way through leathery sausages and pockmarked spuds long after Professor Apocalypse has told us they must be chucked. Alas, not all our fellow countrymen are so sensible. Deep municipal rubbish pits are filled with perfectly edible produce every year. Householders are so browbeaten by authority that they swallow its every word and follow best-before dates with lumpen religiosity. Our belief in 'experts' is touching but sometimes it is hard to escape the suspicion that best-before dates have been selected not by any scientific formula but by a bloke in marketing throwing an arrow at a dartboard, noting the number and trebling it. Look at the best-before date on your bottle of angostura bitters or Worcester sauce. How did they arrive at that particular calculation? Pure guesswork, designed to create a veneer of knowledge and – ideally – a customer who will return to the service counter. The more food that is discarded, the more will be bought afresh. Hoist the sales!

One of the main factories of silliness in this field is the Food Standards Agency, founded by the Blair Government soon after it took office in 1997. It has a big sister in Brussels, the European Food Safety Authority. Number-two item on the information bar at its website? 'Jobs'. Now that may tell us something. Is it a Food Safety Authority or a Job Security Agency? Look at the number of board members it has – enough for a cricket team and appointed on national quotas. Is this really an organisation devoted to the prevention of salmonella poisoning or is it a governmental nursery, a public-sector campsite for trundlers who have paid their dues to the status quo over many years of undistinguished appeasement? These agencies are parking bays for careerists.

Our Food Standards Agency argues that society has the right to inspect the public's diet in order to protect the unhealthy. The Government spends billions on healthcare and one of the causes of poor health is bad eating. The agency is run by ardent big-staters, the sort of people who believe in 'herd immunity' via compulsory inoculation and therefore threaten to rusticate schoolchildren until they have had their arms punctured by the MMR vaccine. They expound 'best practice', the ultimate do-as-I-say creed which denies state employees a chance to use their discretion. Look at their photographs on the websites, read their curricula vitae, examine the language they use in their speeches, and you will find that while they appear to be wizards of the community, often proclaiming professional titles such as 'Dr' or 'Professor', they are in fact figures of immense conformity. Seldom do you find someone who could qualify for the term 'independent-minded', let alone 'self-employed' or 'entrepreneurial' or 'rural-dweller'. Seldom do you find someone who has lived outside the political-scientific think pod. Keeping the system on the go, parroting the departmental line, is therefore in their interest. The question 'Could tax money be saved by shutting us down?' is never asked. Good God, no. The person who mentions 'value for money' at such organisations is regarded as a bad smell in the corner. What we see here is an Establishment as calcified as the Edwardian elite which babyboomers so long attacked. They have all the faults of the 'old-boy network' and few of its virtues of honesty and economy.

There might once have been a case for a government office which checks that the globalised food firms are not slipping us Mickey Finns, but commercially driven lawyers could now do the job perfectly well. No one wants cyanide in the water supply or ground chicken bone in reconstipated – sorry, reconstituted – ham, but with compensation laws as they stand, a firm would have to be pretty damn silly to attempt such behaviour. The Food Standards Agency, ever seeking new powers, strays into areas that are less obviously part of its natural remit. Why should an agency which is meant to supervise food standards take it upon itself to promote Indian curries and Caribbean fruit salads and Jamaican patties in English schools? These may all be tasty and nourishing dishes, but is there another agenda at work here – a joining of multi-cultural hands with the race relations industry? And let our doctors tell us to lose weight and eat more greens if needs must, but food scientists should keep their latex-gloved paws out of such private matters. The zealots again resort to their argument that citizens' health is involved and that the public cost involved is justification for healthy food promotion. Well, let them call it the Diet Propaganda Agency, then, and let them reintroduce daily competitive games in our state schools. The egalitarians would hate that, but it would do far more to improve the nation's health.

Food label laws are enforced under the Food Labelling Regulations 1996 (thank you, John Major) which compel manufacturers to place an 'appropriate durability indication' on all foodstuffs. 'Appropriate' is a loose word. Manufacturers could be more vague about their best-before dates. Is there not a danger that their precision about the very point at which a bag of salt will turn into a health hazard will bring food science into disrepute? Why should anyone believe these people if they so obviously bluff on matters which cannot be known for sure? It is the same with health and safety enforcement. Niggles about bouncy castle rules at garden fêtes imperil the important work done on health and safety at building sites. And yet the Food Standards Agency surges ahead with its enforcement, its didacticism, its director-general making a speech entitled 'Salt: The Challenges and Opportunities'. For goodness' sake, woman, go and plunge your tongue into a good, zingy margarita. Live dangerously.

Food safety labelling is symbolic of a standardising clerical class which no longer asks itself, 'Why should we do this?' Until, that is, June 2010, when Environment Secretary Hilary Benn became the first senior figure to suggest that maybe we should remove best-before dates from certain products. Mr Benn was aghast at the waste of food being binned the moment it passes its best-by date. As the minister responsible not only for agriculture but also rubbish tips, he was worried at the pointlessness of so much landfill. In the Whitehall job-creation world there was an intake of breath at Mr Benn's suggestion. This was the first time any politician had suggested a row-back from ever greater food nannying. Allow the teeming masses to make up their own minds about food safety? Let the British public use their common sense? Good God! An outrage! Thousands of jobs could be put at risk!

Let us most fervently hope so.

Epilogue

Sorry about that. Don't know what came over me. Mind you, a prolonged rant cleans out the arteries. My pipes should be as clear as a fresh-swept chimney.

There is a danger that the reader, clanged over the head by such a prolonged wail, will stagger away in depression. We're all dooooomed. To counter the likely accusations from Establishment trusties that this is an irresponsibly negative work I will close by making ten brief – arguably positive – suggestions. If these were followed, Britain would not be saved overnight. They might, though, delay oblivion by five minutes.

1. Most other education ploys having been tried, open scores of grammar schools in our poorest city centres. Oh, and allow private schools to retain charitable status, the excellence of their education alone being a benefit to the nation.

2. Make Charles Moore chairman of the BBC, giving him instructions to reimpose Reithian virtues. If this results in the departure of Jonathan Ross from the Corporation's airwaves we will all have to be terribly brave and contain our disappointment.

3. Relieve Whitehall of its speechwriters. This would force ministers to write their own speeches. If they continued to

spout gibberish we would then at least know it was *their* gibberish. Exceptions could be made for the Prime Minister, Foreign Secretary and Home Secretary as they are so busy, but there is little reason the rest of the clowns should not sit down and apply themselves. It might mean they made fewer speeches. A boon.

4. Ask the Speaker of the Commons kindly to wear robes and wig – and, while he is about it, to drop his PR man. This would restore an aura of judicial grandeur to the Chair of our elected Chamber.

5. Reduce train announcements to emergencies and to a brief announcement (repeated once) of the station just reached. Any guard who interrupts the peace of a 'quiet carriage' to tell them that it is, indeed, a 'quiet carriage', will be forced to alight from the train at the next stop, there to be left, even if it is raining.

6. Decommission the bureaucracy-mad, grievance-generating, Harman-appeasing Equality and Human Rights Commission, putting all its weapons and squabbling operatives out of use. They will not be able to complain about loss of status because, after all, they believe we are all equal. Let them toil as lavatory cleaners.

7. Reintroduce bus conductors to central London routes.

8. Repeal the law which enabled no-win-no-fee legal deals, the single biggest cause of vexatious health and safety claims. Let us again become a country in which the noun 'suit' refers to an outfit you wear to work.

9. Take Cambridge and Oxford out of the state's maw and allow them to become private universities, selecting undergraduates simply on merit rather than background.

10. Deport Germaine Greer.